WRITERS AND CRITICS

Chief Editor

A. NORMAN JEFFARES

Advisory Editors

DAVID DAICHES

C. P. SNOW

WILLIAM FAULKNER

MICHAEL MILLGATE

CAPRICORN BOOKS
NEW YORK

© Text and Bibliography 1961
Michael Millgate

CAPRICORN BOOKS EDITION, 1971

Published by arrangement with
OLIVER AND BOYD LTD.
Tweeddale Court, Edinburgh 1

First Published 1961
Reprinted 1963
Revised and reprinted 1966
Second Impression

Library of Congress Catalog
Card Number: 79-172988

Printed in the United States of America

CONTENTS

ACKNOWLEDGMENTS

Acknowledgments are due to Chatto and Windus Ltd, and to the following American publishers for permission to reproduce quotations from the works of William Faulkner: Liveright Publishing Corporation (*Mosquitoes, Soldiers' Pay*); Random House, Inc. (*Absalom, Absalom!, As I Lay Dying, Go Down, Moses, A Green Bough, The Hamlet, Light in August, Pylon, Sanctuary, Sartoris, The Sound and the Fury, The Unvanquished, The Wild Palms*).

Acknowledgments are also due to the following for permission to quote from the works indicated: Cassell and Co. Ltd (Wyndham Lewis, *Men Without Art*); Houghton Mifflin Company (Maxwell Geismar, *Writers in Crisis*); *New Republic* (article by Robert Penn Warren); Mr George M. O'Donnell and *Kenyon Review* (article by George M. O'Donnell); Mr Irving Howe (Irving Howe, *William Faulkner: A Critical Study*); Martin Secker and Warburg, Ltd, and Viking Press, Inc. (*Writers at Work: The Paris Review Interviews*, ed. Malcolm Cowley); Mr Malcolm Cowley and Viking Press, Inc. (*The Portable Faulkner*, ed. Malcolm Cowley).

The photograph on the front cover is reproduced by permission of Ralph Thompson.

M.M.

ABBREVIATED TITLES USED IN THE TEXT

In all references to Faulkner's works, the first of the two page-references normally given is to the American edition, the second (in brackets) to the English edition, listed in the Bibliography (below, pp. 117–20) as standard.

A.A.	=	*Absalom, Absalom!*
A.D.	=	*As I Lay Dying*
G.D.M.	=	*Go Down, Moses*
H.	=	*The Hamlet*
L.A.	=	*Light in August*
M.	=	*Mosquitoes*
R.N.	=	*Requiem for a Nun*
S.	=	*Sanctuary*
S.F.	=	*The Sound and the Fury*
W.P.	=	*The Wild Palms*
F.U.	=	*Faulkner in the University*, ed. Frederick L. Gwynn and Joseph L. Blotner
P.F.	=	*The Portable Faulkner*, ed. Malcolm Cowley
T.D.C.	=	*William Faulkner: Two Decades of Criticism*, ed. Frederick J. Hoffman and Olga W. Vickery
W.W.	=	*Writers at Work*, ed. Malcolm Cowley

CHAPTER I

FAULKNER AND MISSISSIPPI

Oxford, Mississippi, county seat of Lafayette County and site of the University of Mississippi, is a town of some four thousand inhabitants lying about seventy-five miles south-east of Memphis, Tennessee, and just to the east of the low rich cotton lands of the Mississippi Delta. It is hill country here, the land eroded into deep gulches, and many of the county's inhabitants are poor white or Negro tenant farmers living in ramshackle cabins along dirt roads and scraping the barest of livings from the meagre soil. In the countryside, where buzzards wheel and Negro children run for home at the sight of white men in a car, the road passes the huts and roofed-in prayer benches of camp-meeting grounds where revival meetings are held or the remains of once-prosperous towns long since dis-appeared—College Hill, for example, at one time Oxford's rival, now marked by little more than a dilapidated store and a handsome church, built by slaves and with traces of the old slave gallery still clearly visible.

The town itself is quiet, almost drowsy, coming alive only on Saturday afternoons, when local farmers still bring their produce into town and sell it from the backs of station-wagons or pick-up trucks, and one side of the square becomes black with Negro faces. The square, of course, is the centre of things: here stands the heavy white county courthouse, the statue of the Confederate soldier facing steadfastly to the South, the old-fashioned wooden shop-fronts, some of them still with projecting first-floor verandahs which overhang the pavements and shade loungers and passers-by from the oppressive heat of the

Southern sun. On the outskirts of town the ubiquitous ranch-type houses are going up in the new developments, and the shops on the square are full of nationally-advertised goods; but Oxford, in common with much of Mississippi, still appears to the European eye less "modern" than almost any part of the United States outside the Indian reservations of the South-West. The most vivid visual impressions one can take away from the town—the elegance of the pre-Civil-War houses and the abysmal squalor of some of the Negro dwellings—offer the most violent contrast, yet both are a direct inheritance of that Southern past, at once proud and shameful, of which Oxford, more even than most Southern towns, is so vividly aware.

One of the things that has caused Oxford to be particularly aware of its past is the fact that it was for more than fifty years the home of William Faulkner, at once the most deeply Southern of Southern writers and the only one who has yet achieved a genuinely international reputation. Oxford was for many years indifferent to its literary fame, but the controversy aroused by *Intruder in the Dust*, the excitement consequent upon its being filmed on location in Oxford itself, and, above all, the award to Faulkner of the Nobel Prize for Literature, have done a good deal to force him upon the town's attention and respect. Although Faulkner now spends much of his time in Charlottesville, Virginia, Oxford and the surrounding region are intimately bound up with his experience as a man and as a writer, and they occupy a central position in the whole body of his work.

At the heart of Faulkner's work, the setting and scene of most of his novels, is his legendary Yoknapatawpha County. It is supposed to be in north-western Mississippi, with its county seat, called Jefferson, lying about seventy-five miles south-east of Memphis and forty miles from Oxford, the site of the state university. Most of the countryside consists of low pine-covered hills, cut into deep gullies by erosion. To the north of the county lies the Tallahatchie River, where General Compson has his hunting camp. To the south is the Yoknapatawpha River from which the county takes its name, and nearby is Frenchman's Bend, with the Old Frenchman place, setting of *The Hamlet* and much of *Sanctuary*. North and south through the county runs John Sartoris's railway. We gather these details, and a great many more, from the novels themselves—although they are not always consistent one with another—and from the maps which Faulkner has drawn from time to time: on the one he drew for *Absalom, Absalom!* in 1936 he wrote, "William Faulkner, Sole Owner and Proprietor." Both sources make it abundantly clear that the Jefferson and Yoknapatawpha County of Faulkner's legend are based closely upon the Oxford and Lafayette County of geographical fact.

Oxford and Jefferson are exactly the same distance from Memphis in exactly the same direction, and many features of the two towns coincide—down to the position of the Confederate monument which plays such an important part on the last page of *The Sound and the Fury*—but it is impossible to say categorically that Jefferson *is* Oxford. Not only has Faulkner moved away the state university, but Yoknapatawpha County is much bigger than the actual Lafayette County—apparently to give Faulkner space to get everything in, including the one hundred square miles of Thomas Sutpen's plantation described in *Absalom, Absalom!*—and its population is at once smaller and more Negro: population figures given by Faulkner on his map of 1936 show a 3 : 2 ratio between Negroes and whites, whereas the actual county seems always to have had a slight majority of whites. These statistics, and others, are given by Ward L. Miner in his study *The World of William Faulkner*; and Miner is no doubt correct in suggesting that these modifications were designed by Faulkner to make Jefferson more generally typical of northern Mississippi.[1]

The world of Faulkner's novels is not that of Lafayette County but that of Yoknapatawpha County, a quite different place—a "mythical kingdom," as Malcolm Cowley calls it,[2] of which Faulkner is "sole owner and proprietor." At the same time, Metro-Goldwyn-Mayer were right to go to Oxford to make their film of *Intruder in the Dust*. Faulkner's personal world is undoubtedly that of Lafayette County, his home, the source and scene of most of his experiences from early boyhood until late middle-age; and if Jefferson is not Oxford in any precise sense, it is only out of Faulkner's knowledge of Oxford that Jefferson could be created. Faulkner's preoccupation with the South in the great majority of his novels seems a product less of his will than of his environment: for Faulkner, as a Southerner intensely aware of the past of his own region and of his own family, the South was not merely an obvious subject for his fiction but, fiercely and inescapably, the inevitable subject.

The history of Faulkner's own family was dominated by the figure of his great-grandfather, Colonel William Cuthbert Falkner. (William, the novelist, has resumed the "u" which is said to have been in the original spelling of the family name, but he, too, was born Falkner.) Colonel Falkner was an extraordinary man who was still in the novelist's youth a vivid and often awesome memory in the countryside, and the subject of numerous local and family legends. Despite the recent researches of Robert Cantwell,[3] the Colonel's violent early career in Ripley, Miss., is still somewhat mysterious. It is enough to say here that he was born in 1825, fought in the Mexican War, was twice tried for murder and twice acquitted, and played a considerable part in local politics as a leader of the Know-Nothing Party—an anti-Catholic, anti-foreign, secret society which was temporarily an important force in American politics during the eighteen-fifties.

When the Civil War began, Falkner raised his own company, the Magnolia Rifles of Tippah County, was elected Colonel of the Second Infantry of the Confederate States Army, and led them at the battle of Bull Run. In the spring of 1862, however, his troops elected a new colonel, and Falkner returned to Ripley, where he organised a cavalry regiment and later served with it under General Nathan Bedford Forrest. After the Civil War, Falkner built a narrow-gauge railway, with sixty miles of track and two engines, and dreamed of extending it to the Gulf of Mexico. He also ran a large plantation and various other business enterprises, founded a college, and wrote a play, a book of travels, and two novels—one of which, *The White Rose of Memphis*, was a considerable popular success.

On 5 Nov. 1889, Colonel Falkner was elected to the Mississippi state legislature, and on the same day he was shot on the square at Ripley by J. H. Thurmond, his former partner in the building of the railway, who had become both political rival and bitter personal enemy. Thurmond was tried for murder, acquitted after a sensational trial, and left for North Carolina, where he later made a fortune in textiles. The Falkners also moved away from Ripley, but stayed in Mississippi, arriving in Oxford around 1900. They had sold the railway, and the Colonel's son, who acquired by inheritance the courtesy title of "the Young Colonel," was at one time Assistant United States District Attorney for Northern Mississippi. His son, Murry C. Falkner, the novelist's father, eventually became business manager for the University of Mississippi, but was earlier employed as a conductor on the railway. The family seems never to have been badly off, but it is clear that William Faulkner has had cause to be aware, within his own family, of the classic Southern experience of a glamorous and more or less prosperous past contrasted with a relatively constricted present: the family, like the region, is poor where it was once rich, and the people themselves seem somehow smaller than once they were. Almost every novel of Faulkner's in some way exploits and explores this contrast, and, as often as not, in terms of his own family.

Just as it is impossible to identify Jefferson with Oxford completely, it is an exaggeration to say, as some critics have done, that the Sartorises of Faulkner's novels *are* the members of his own family. There can be no doubt, however, that Colonel Falkner is, in large degree, the original of Colonel John Sartoris of *Sartoris*, *The Unvanquished*, and, more briefly, of several other novels. Anyone who has read *Sartoris* and *The Unvanquished* will realise at once that many incidents in these books—the building of the railway, for example, the demotion of Sartoris from his first command, the shooting of Sartoris by Redmond—are based closely upon fact, or upon the legendary versions of original facts that Faulkner himself must have heard (Cantwell recalls Faulkner's saying that he had never read any history but simply picked it up from talking to people).[4] It is no accident that *Sartoris*, the book in which we see the first signs of Faulkner's mature manner, is to a remarkable degree a collection of re-worked family characters, anecdotes and legends, with perhaps even a touch of autobiography in the presentation of young Bayard. Faulkner's own family history first got him started as a writer, and his deep Mississippi roots have sustained him ever since.

Faulkner himself[5] was born on 25 Sept. 1897, at New Albany (about thirty-five miles from Oxford), the eldest of the four sons of Murry C. Falkner and his wife, Maud Butler of Oxford. The family moved to Oxford while Faulkner was still a child, and it was there that he grew up and went to school. He made no particular impression upon either neighbours or teachers and left high school without graduating. He seems at first to have done little but wander about and read without much sense of purpose or direction, but in 1914 began his friendship with Phil Stone, who already had degrees from the University of Mississippi and from Yale. Stone, four years his senior, told him what to read, talked with him about literature and about the South, and encouraged and criticised his writing, which at that time and for some time afterwards was mostly verse.

When the United States entered the First World War, Faulkner, unable to join the American army, joined the Royal Air Force in Canada and began training as a pilot. Despite the legends that have grown up around him, he never went to Europe. Back in Oxford after the war he seems to have devoted himself for a time to the cultivation of mild eccentricities. For a short while he attended the University of Mississippi, doing quite well in Spanish and French but failing disastrously in English. Late in 1920, at the invitation of Stark Young, who was also from northern Mississippi, he made his first visit to New York. He worked in a book-shop for a time, but the only useful result of the trip seems to have been his friendship with Elizabeth Prall, whose marriage to Sherwood Anderson was to give Faulkner his first introduction to a really lively literary circle. For the moment, however, Faulkner returned to Oxford to become university postmaster. He is said to have discharged the functions of that office with notable inefficiency and, on the occasion of his dismissal or resignation (the evidence is conflicting), to have declared that at least he would no longer be at the beck and call of anyone who happened to have two cents for a stamp.

By this time he had published several poems in the University's year-book and in its newspaper, *The Mississippean*, and one each in the *New Republic* and the New Orleans "little magazine," the *Double Dealer*; and in 1924, the year the postmastership ended, Phil Stone financed the private publication of a small volume of Faulkner's verse entitled *The Marble Faun*. This was Faulkner's first experience of book-publication, and an unhappy one, for the book attracted few sales and little attention. Shortly afterwards he set off for New Orleans, where he intended to take a boat to Europe. But he met Sherwood Anderson (married by now to Elizabeth Prall), and stayed on in the city for six months, enjoying his first experience of literary society and publishing sketches in the *Times-Picayune* newspaper and in the *Double Dealer*. Anderson, at this time, was at the height of his reputation, and the recognition and encouragement he gave Faulkner was an extremely important factor in the younger man's career. It seems to have been largely Anderson's influence that turned Faulkner to fiction, and it was certainly Anderson who helped him publish his first novel, *Soldiers' Pay*, which he wrote during the New Orleans visit.

Anderson was by no means Faulkner's only friend in New Orleans, however, and with one of the others, the artist William Spratling, Faulkner collaborated in the production of *Sherwood Anderson & other Famous Creoles* published in New Orleans at the end of 1926. This little book of fifty-one pages was primarily a collection of Spratling's drawings, but Faulkner contributed a brief introduction, signed "W.F.," in a parody of Anderson's rather uneven literary style. The exercise was much milder and much less extended than Hemingway's parody of Anderson in *The Torrents of Spring*, published the same year, but Anderson was offended and broke off his friendship with Faulkner, though he continued to speak highly of him as a writer. In the meantime Faulkner had gone to Europe with Spratling in July 1925. He visited northern Italy, spent some time in Paris without becoming converted to the current fashion of expatriation, and returned to the United States in December.

Soldiers' Pay was published by Liveright early in 1926, and had a mild critical success. The book sold poorly, but Liveright signed a contract for a second novel, *Mosquitoes*, which was written at Pascagoula, on the Gulf coast of Mississippi, during 1926 and published early in

1927. The reviews were less favourable than those of *Soldiers' Pay*, even fewer copies of the book were sold, and the publisher's contract was not renewed. Despite this setback, Faulkner continued to write, living at home in Oxford and picking up a little money here and there by doing odd jobs. In Faulkner's introduction to the Modern Library edition of *Sanctuary*, published in 1932, he speaks of painting houses and carpentering, and of a job on the night-shift at the town power plant shovelling coal for the boilers. Faulkner says that on this job, using the slack hours between midnight and 4 a.m., and working on a table contrived from a wheel-barrow, he was able to write *As I Lay Dying* in six weeks during the summer of 1929.[6]

It was in 1929 that Faulkner married Estelle Oldham, an Oxford girl whom he had known for many years and who had two children by a previous marriage; and the year was an important one in his life for other reasons as well. In January, Harcourt, Brace published *Sartoris*, after Liveright had turned it down. Sales were again low, but in writing the book Faulkner had made important discoveries about himself and his region. He later told Robert Cantwell that when he was half-way through the book, " 'suddenly I discovered that writing was a mighty fine thing—you could make people stand on their hind legs and cast a shadow.' "[7] More recently still, he told an interviewer for the *Paris Review*:

With *Soldiers' Pay* and *Mosquitoes* I wrote for the sake of writing because it was fun. Beginning with *Sartoris* I discovered that my own little postage stamp of native soil was worth writing about and that I would never live long enough to exhaust it, and that by sublimating the actual into the apocryphal I would have complete liberty to use whatever talent I might have to its absolute top. It opened up a gold mine of other people, so I created a cosmos of my own.[8]

The astonishing outcome of this discovery—astonishing in its own right, still more astonishing when seen against the background of his earlier novels—was *The Sound and the Fury*, published in October 1929 by Jonathan Cape and Harrison Smith. Critical reception of *The Sound and the Fury* was mixed, but it was always respectful and sometimes warm. Faulkner, who for the first time had "written [his] guts"[9] into a book without worrying about whether or not it would sell, had also received his first important encouragement from beyond the circle of his own acquaintance.

From this time onwards he seems to have devoted himself to writing—despite his favourite habit of telling interviewers he is essentially a farmer who writes for fun—and his adoption of professional status was made memorable by the publication of his sensational novel *Sanctuary*. The sensationalism, according to Faulkner's own account in the introduction to the Modern Library edition, was entirely deliberate. His previous novels had brought him a certain amount of critical praise but little financial reward: now he would write a book expressly designed to make money. Faulkner says that he "invented the most horrific tale I could imagine," wrote it out in three weeks or so, and sent it straight off to his publisher, though he extensively revised the book before it was finally published by Cape and Smith in February 1931.[10]

Sanctuary certainly shocked its readers—nowhere more obviously than in Oxford itself—but it was undoubtedly a popular success. It made Faulkner the money he needed. It made him, too, a popular reputation of a kind he had never expected and did not particularly want. Paramount bought the story and made from it a film called *The Story of Temple Drake*, and from this time dates Faulkner's long, legendary and mutually profitable relationship with Hollywood.

In the 'thirties and 'forties Faulkner made several visits to Hollywood lasting weeks or months at a time and worked as script-writer on a variety of films including those of Hemingway's *To Have and to Have Not* and Raymond Chandler's *The Big Sleep*. Anecdotes of his Hollywood visits abound: there is a collection of them in the eighth chapter of Robert Coughlan's *The Private World of William Faulkner*, and Faulkner gave his own version of some of them in his *Paris Review* interview with Jean Stein. The world of Hollywood has had unfortunate effects upon a good many American writers who have been attracted there. That Faulkner has escaped these effects seems to be largely due to his refusal to become involved in Hollywood social life and to his acceptance of script-writing as neither an artistic challenge nor a way of life, but as a short-term job of craftsmanship to be done honestly and then left behind. Faulkner seems to have thoroughly disliked Hollywood itself, and one of the best-known stories about him tells of his asking the studio if he could work at home for a while, and of his employers' horror at receiving, some time later, a card bearing the postmark "Oxford, Mississippi."[11]

Faulkner's sole reason for going to Hollywood was to make money. In the early 'thirties he purchased a handsome house built before the Civil War, and this involved him in heavy expenses. His fondness for flying was also costly, though he gave this up almost completely after the death of his youngest brother Dean in a flying accident in 1935. Another expense was his attachment to strong drink: Coughlan describes in some detail what he calls Faulkner's "alcoholic holidays from reality."[12] Faulkner did not pursue the vein of *Sanctuary*, and his next books sold comparatively few copies. From 1930 onwards he was selling stories to the magazines at a fairly steady rate—in 1934, for example, he placed four stories with the *Saturday Evening Post*, one each with *Harper's*, *Scribners'* and *American Mercury*, and two elsewhere—but his occasional trips to Hollywood provided a useful supplementary income.

Apart from these visits, and business trips to New York to see his publisher, Faulkner seems rarely to have moved from Oxford during the 'thirties and 'forties. He and his wife lost their first child, but they have a second daughter, Jill, and Mrs Faulkner's two children lived at home until they married and left Oxford. His family, the old house, the small farm, and his writing, seemed at one time to occupy the whole of Faulkner's life. For many years he lived in Oxford in something like seclusion, refusing to be interviewed, rarely engaging in correspondence, apparently not even writing a great deal. Between *The Hamlet*, published in 1940 and *Intruder in the Dust*, published in 1948, Faulkner's only book was *Go Down, Moses*, 1942, mostly made up of previously-published short stories—though some of them were extensively revised.

Intruder in the Dust, a novel with overt social and political intentions, heralded a new phase of Faulkner's career as a writer, and he has since published four new novels as well as a number of other books. It also heralded a new development in his relationship with the world, which became even more marked following the award of the Nobel Prize. His famous address on the occasion of the Nobel Prize ceremonies in Stockholm in 1950 has been the forerunner of a remarkable number of speeches, articles, letters to newspapers, and other public statements, in which he has forcibly expressed his views on the past, present, and future of the South, the United States, and the human race. He has made public appearances on several occasions and has travelled abroad a good deal, notably to Europe and Japan.

To make the break with his former life even more decisive, Faulkner now seems to regard Oxford as only partly his home and goes annually to Charlottesville, Virginia, where the University of Virginia is situated. And, as writer-in-residence at the University, this formerly retiring man has not only submitted himself to a series of study-sessions, in which he discussed his work with students, but allowed these sessions to be recorded on tape and then published, in an edited version, under the title *Faulkner in the University*.

The contrasts between the Faulkner of this last stage and the Faulkner of legend add a final twist to the already difficult problem of describing him as a man. The evidence of those who know him is highly contradictory. We find him described in one place as pleasant in manner, in another as stiff; as warm, and coldly reserved; as modest, and fiercely proud; as courteous, and capable of insult; as a kind and thoughtful friend and father, and as a man with a streak of intolerance and even of cruelty. It need not greatly worry us, however, that Faulkner remains for the moment an enigmatic figure. His books offer enigmas enough, and the puzzling personality of their author may safely be left for his biographers to unravel. It seems quite possible that he is a far simpler man than his readers are at present ready to believe. The novels themselves are not simple, and are unlikely ever to seem so, but they are among the great books of the twentieth century. And that is what matters.

REFERENCES

1. Miner, *The World of William Faulkner* ([1959]), p. 88.

2. *P.F.*, p. 5.

3. This paragraph and the two following are based on Cantwell, Introduction to *Sartoris* (Signet edition, 1953).

4. Cantwell, "The Faulkners: Recollections of a Gifted Family," *New World Writing 2* (1952), p. 306.

5. There is no biography of Faulkner as yet. The outline of his life in this chapter is particularly indebted to Cantwell, "The Faulkners . . .," Robert Coughlan, *The Private World of William Faulkner* (1954), and William Van O'Connor, *The Tangled Fire of William Faulkner* (1954).

6. *S.*, p. vii.

7. Cantwell, *New World Writing*
   2, p. 306.

8. *W.W.*, p. 141.

9. *S.*, p. vi.

10. *S.*, pp. vi–viii.

11. Coughlan, *The Private World*
    of William Faulkner, p. 111.

12. *Op. cit.*, p. 104 (cp. pp. 24–
    25).

CHAPTER II

APPRENTICESHIP AND ACHIEVEMENT

Faulkner is a difficult novelist, and for this reason his books will be considered here one by one, as separate entities, rather than as amorphous segments of a larger whole. It may be as well to suggest at this point, however, that the real difficulties of Faulkner's work do not lie in that provinciality of his which English readers sometimes regard as such a barrier. If it is a barrier, it is an extremely flimsy one and one which we have erected ourselves. The feeling that without knowing the American South we cannot come to terms with the South's supreme novelist is largely a product of our awareness of the acute racial problems of the South today and of our natural inclination to seek in Faulkner's work some interpretation of this situation. Though there is no doubt that Faulkner has been acutely and even explicitly aware of these problems, especially in his later work, it is a mistake to let his Southernness bulk too large.

Although Faulkner's setting may be provincial, his major and most persistent themes are universally relevant, and, in a sense, all that we need to know about the South is contained in the novels themselves. It does not greatly matter to us, as readers of literature, whether or not Faulkner's portrait of the South is an accurate one— whether, to borrow a phrase from Allen Tate, it is true what he says about Dixie.[1] A young writer who lives in Oxford—since Faulkner, Eudora Welty, Stark Young, and the rest, writers are thick on the ground in Mississippi—was sternly warned by a local lady, soon after the publication of his first novel, "not to go around misrepresentin' Mississippi like that Mr. Faulkner." On the surface, of course, Faulkner does misrepresent Mississippi. The day-to-day life of the South is a good deal more peaceful than we might sometimes assume from reading the more violent of his novels. But Faulkner's best work is not so much a portrait of the South as an image of its predicament; and without being "true to life" in the strict sociological sense it may nevertheless strike home to the inner truths of the Southern mind—and of the human heart.

There is little that is especially Southern about Faulkner's early writing. He began as a poet—and still likes to think of himself as one—and his verse seems to belong less to any native tradition than to the world of London in the eighteen-nineties. Despite occasional felicities, it is not particularly good verse, even of its kind, but it has considerable interest as giving us some idea of where Faulkner started from as a writer. The most important collection of Faulkner's poems is *A Green Bough* (1933), and, with the recent appearance of a French bilingual edition, this is the only one readily accessible in England. *The Marble Faun* seems to be unobtainable, so does *Salmagundi* (1932), a small volume of Faulkner's contributions to the *Double Dealer*.

Readers of the novels, however, will be familiar with the fragments of verse first published in *Soldiers' Pay* and *Mosquitoes* and subsequently incorporated, after some revisions, into *A Green Bough*, and these fragments alone are sufficient to give some impression of the general tone and manner of Faulkner's verse. Here, for example, is *A Green Bough*, XXXVIII, revised from *Mosquitoes* (p. 252), where it is given the title "Hermaphroditus":

Lips that of thy weary all seem weariest,
And wearier for the curled and pallid sly
Still riddle of thy secret face, and thy
Sick despair of its own ill obsessed;

Lay no hand to heart, do not protest
That smiling leaves thy tired mouth reconciled,
For swearing so keeps thee but ill beguiled
With secret joy of thine own flank and breast.

Weary thy mouth with smiling: canst thou bride
Thyself with thee, or thine own kissing slake?
Thy belly's waking doth itself deride
With sleep's sharp absence, coming so awake;
And near thy mouth thy twinned heart's grief doth hide
For there's no breast between: it cannot break.[2]

Among the most obvious elements in this sonnet are the touches of *fin-de-siècle* "weariness" and eroticism and the suggestions of "Elizabethanising" in the diction and movement, and perhaps in the very choice of the sonnet form. Throughout the poems Swinburne is the most pervasive influence, but there are frequent echoes of Shakespeare and other Elizabethan writers—as in *A Green Bough*, XVI, which is also interesting for its anticipation of some aspects of the Quentin section of *The Sound and the Fury*. In individual poems the influence of more recent writers is immediately apparent: Housman in XI, XII and XIII, for instance; E. E. Cummings in IV; T. S. Eliot in I and XXVII.

The Eliot who influenced Faulkner seems to be the Eliot of the poems previous to *The Waste Land*, particularly of "The Love Song of J. Alfred Prufrock" and the Sweeney poems. This is one of many indications that all of Faulkner's verse belongs to a very early period in his career. Harry Runyan tells us that the text of *The Marble Faun*, published in 1924, is dated 1919, and that *A Green Bough*, was announced for publication as early as February 1925.[3] Faulkner published no poems in magazines between 1925 and 1932, when *Contempo*, a Southern "little magazine," ran a special Faulkner issue which included nine previously-unpublished poems. Five of these reappeared, slightly revised, in *A Green Bough*, as—this time without revision—did six poems published in the *New Republic* in 1933, just about the time the book appeared. We hear of sonnets dated from Pascagoula in 1926, but it seems extremely likely that soon after he had turned to fiction in the middle 'twenties Faulkner gave up poetry altogether.

Faulkner's first fiction was published, and presumably written, during his six months stay in New Orleans in 1925. It consisted of a series of sketches, mainly descriptive of New Orleans life, which appeared in the *Double Dealer* and the *Times-Picayune* newspaper, and which have recently been collected by Carvel Collins under the title *New Orleans Sketches* (1958). Several of the sketches, notably the eleven entitled "New Orleans" (contributed to the *Double Dealer*), are exercises in impressionistic prose of a kind which suggests the presence of the same late-Romantic, *fin-de-siècle* influences that were evident in Faulkner's verse. More interesting are some of the longer pieces for the *Times-Picayune*: for all their weaknesses of construction and style, stories like "The Liar" and "Country Mice," for example, do look forward to the narrative manner of Faulkner's best work in the short-story form. Collins in his introduction points out the first appearance in some of the sketches of themes and motifs that become of great importance in Faulkner's later work,[4] and it must be said of all these early pieces that, like the poems, they are interesting not for their own sakes but for the incidental hints of future greatness they happen to contain.

The first work of Faulkner's that is interesting and important in its own right is the novel *Soldiers' Pay*, which was published in America in 1926 but did not appear in England until 1930. *Soldiers' Pay* is the work of a young and gifted minor novelist: it is hard to realise, at first, that it was written by the same man who, only three years later, wrote *The Sound and the Fury*. The difference between *Soldiers' Pay*, though an extremely impressive first novel, and Faulkner's mature work is not merely one of quality, but of kind. The dominating influence here is that of Aldous Huxley—at times it seems to go back beyond Huxley to Peacock himself—and the style is highly self-conscious and rather precious, relying a good deal on a purely verbal wit and, in its more ambitious moments, on rhythmic patterns strongly reminiscent of Swinburne. Now and then we catch suggestions of the early poems of T. S. Eliot. This evocation of a spring evening, for example, owes something to "Rhapsody on a Windy Night":

Nine-thirty

People sat on porches rocking and talking in low tones, enjoying the warmth of April, people passing beneath dark trees along the street, old and young, men and women, making comfortable, unintelligible sounds, like cattle going to barn and bed. Tiny red eyes passed along at mouth-height and burning tobacco lingered behind sweet and pungent. Spitting arc lights, at street corners, revealed the passers-by, temporarily dogging them with elastic shadows. . . .[5]

It is the unexpected simile, "like cattle going to barn and bed," that betrays the essential Faulkner lurking beneath the late-Romantic manner.

Like John Dos Passos's *Three Soldiers* (1921), *Soldiers' Pay* is a novel of post-war bitterness and disillusionment: the tragic figure of Donald Mahon, suffering his living death, is set against the comic satyr figure of Januarius Jones, the quintessential civilian, whose highly extraverted sexual behaviour expresses rather than denies his spiritual deadness. As we read the novel, however, we become increasingly aware that it is, in a very particular sense, a novel about the South; from its contrived passages of impressionistic description a picture of a small Southern town does gradually and imperfectly emerge.

It is called Charlestown and it is in Georgia, but in its blurred outlines we may now recognise the preliminary sketches for Jefferson, Mississippi. Looking back at *Soldiers' Pay* with the later novels in mind we can also see several Faulkner character-types already present in embryonic form. Mahon, the World War I flier whose life stopped at the moment he was shot down, anticipates young Bayard Sartoris of *Sartoris* and the many stories about flying during and after the war; Cecily Saunders, who is engaged to Mahon but eventually deserts him, looks forward to Temple Drake and Little Belle of *Sanctuary* and to all Faulkner's other pretty, trivial, self-centred, dangerously innocent Southern girls; while Cecily's parents are in some ways early versions of Mr and Mrs Compson of *The Sound and the Fury*.

There also appear in this first novel of Faulkner's the bare hints of techniques which are to be much more fully and audaciously developed in later books: the slight but noticeable emphasis on time, for example, the interest in the widely differing reactions of different characters to the same event—here the return of Mahon in his dead-alive state—and, especially in Ch. 5, the attempt to explore these differences by presenting and juxtaposing the characters' inner thoughts. But if the book makes structural gestures in the direction of *As I Lay Dying*, it is still a very long way from the assurance and control of Faulkner's mature work. The sophistication of Huxley offered a highly seductive model for young writers in the 'twenties, and it provided Faulkner with a useful jumping-off point, it enabled him to get started. Yet it was not his natural manner, and Huxley's influence—like the very different influence of Sherwood Anderson, whose writing of the *Dark Laughter* period is reflected in the Negro church episode at the end of the book—was something that Faulkner had to work his way out of before he could properly find himself as a writer.

In Faulkner's second novel, *Mosquitoes* (1927), however,

the influence of Huxley is even more marked. The whole novel is a 'twenties "period piece" of a highly self-conscious kind which takes up and develops some of the weakest aspects of its predecessor. In *Soldiers' Pay* the moving story of Donald Mahon, though imperfectly handled, provides the kind of firm core which *Mosquitoes* so obviously lacks. All that happens in the later book is that a group of New Orleans artists, "art-lovers," and hangers-on go for a cruise on a yacht and talk. Although various people go through the rituals of flirtation, and an attempted elopement is foiled by the discouraging activities of the swamp mosquitoes, the bulk of the book is taken up with heavy conversation about such topics as art, life, beauty, and sex.

There are signs throughout the book that part of Faulkner's intention is to demonstrate the futility of talk —Gordon, the one genuine artist, is the least talkative of all the characters, while the comic and perpetually frustrated Mr Talliaferro is the strongest believer in the efficacy of words—but Faulkner fails to solve the old problem of how to present boring characters without boring the reader. The author's voice sometimes interposes such comments as, "Talk, talk, talk: the utter and heartbreaking stupidity of words,"[6] but this apparent attempt on Faulkner's part to dissociate himself from his work is far more likely to exasperate the reader than to reconcile him to the novel's dullness.

Mosquitoes is interesting today only in so far as it marks a stage in Faulkner's development and hints at the greatness to come. Such hints are fewer and vaguer than in *Soldiers' Pay* but they undoubtedly exist. Jenny, for example, lovely, mindless and passive, looks forward to Lena Grove of *Light in August* and Eula Varner of *The Hamlet*, while Gordon's final remark—" 'Only an idiot has no grief; only a fool would forget it. What else is there in this world sharp enough to stick to your guts?' "[7]—anticipates what is to become a major theme in *The Sound and the Fury* and elsewhere. The liveliest part of the whole book is the splendid "tall tale" about the evolution of one Al Jackson from sheep-farmer to "fish-rancher,"[8] and it is told by the most completely realised of the characters, Dawson Fairchild, whom Faulkner modelled on Sherwood Anderson. Some of the remarks made about Fairchild by other passengers on the yacht contain quite shrewd observations on Anderson's work and on literature in general:

> "Life everywhere is the same, you know. Manners of living it may be different—are they not different between adjoining villages? family names, profits on a single field or orchard, work influences—but man's old compulsions, duty and inclination: the axis and the circumference of his squirrel cage, they do not change...."[9]

Thinking over what he had written about Anderson, Faulkner may have come to realise its relevance to his own problems as a writer. Certainly this passage might stand as an epigraph to the whole "Yoknapatawpha County" sequence, and if it is a fair sample of the direction Faulkner's thoughts were taking at this time, it is not surprising that in his next book he abandons the novel of ideas and plunges into the midst of Jefferson, Mississippi.

Coming to *Sartoris* (1929) after *Soldiers' Pay* and *Mosquitoes* we are immediately aware of a new note in Faulkner's writing:

> As usual, old man Falls had brought John Sartoris into the room with him, had walked the three miles in from the county Poor Farm, fetching, like an odor, like the clean dusty smell of his faded overalls, the spirit of the dead man into that room where the dead man's son sat and where the two of them, pauper and banker, would sit for a half an hour in the company of him who had passed beyond death and then returned.[10]

This is the whole of the opening paragraph, and from our present perspective we recognise here—in the obsession with time, death, and the omnipresence of the past, and in the complexity of the syntax allied with the relative simplicity of the language—the first appearance of Faulkner's mature manner. Later in the book we find passages which betray a lingering attachment to that "aesthetic," Swinburnian interest in language for its own sake which weakened the earlier novels and which in this novel is satirised in the presentation of Horace Benbow. There is no doubt, however, that *Sartoris* marks an extremely important step in Faulkner's development, overshadowed though it is by the much greater achievement of *The Sound and the Fury*, which followed so shortly afterwards.

In *Sartoris* Faulkner discovered both his major theme and the way in which that theme could best be approached; he began the long exploitation of his "little postage stamp of native soil."[11] In *Soldiers' Pay*, Faulkner did a preliminary sketch of a small Southern town, though he placed it in Georgia. In *Sartoris*, Jefferson, Mississippi, makes its appearance for the first time, and it appears already fully grown. The book is rich in characters, settings, and themes which are to be taken up and developed in many later novels and stories, as if, even at this early stage, Faulkner already had a clear vision, not merely in general outline but in detail, of what he intended to do in the whole Yoknapatawpha sequence.

The Sartorises themselves, of course, are to reappear again and again; so are Flem and Byron Snopes, Horace and Narcissa Benbow, Belle Mitchell, Doctor Peabody, the MacCallums, and various minor characters. We begin with *Sartoris*, in fact, that complex and controversial process by which the knowledge of a character obtained in one Faulkner novel inevitably affects our estimation of his behaviour in another novel—as with Horace Benbow's reappearance in *Sanctuary*, for example—while, on the other hand, we may have to go to another work to satisfy our aroused curiosity about a particular character or incident. Thus we must read the story "There was a Queen" to find out what happens to Miss Jenny Du Pre and to the letters which Byron Snopes wrote to Narcissa. Unfortunately, the very richness of *Sartoris* as a kind of source-book for subsequent stories of Jefferson and its region is closely related to its comparative failure as a novel. It is too episodic, lacking a sufficiently strong central core, and the narrative line is too easily deflected into descriptive, elegiac, or comic set-pieces: some of the hunting-scenes, for example, despite their function in the story of young Bayard; the well-known passage about the mule; and a good deal of the rather facile comedy centring on old Simon, the Negro coachman.

The main thread running through the novel is the story of young Bayard Sartoris, grandson of old Bayard the banker, great-grandson of Colonel John Sartoris. It is Colonel John, the character based on Faulkner's grandfather, whose image is invoked in the opening paragraph and throughout the book, so that he becomes a kind of brooding presence, "passed beyond death and then returned." Young Bayard's story consists mainly of his repeated attempts to get himself killed, and it is one of the weaknesses of the novel that the pressures driving him are never made entirely clear. Among them, however, are obviously his passionate love for his twin brother John, who had been shot down over France in 1918, and his oppressive sense of an almost ritualistic obligation to die a "Sartoris" death. In confronting and attempting to understand the violence, confusion, and deprivation of one war, young Bayard is confused and hemmed in by the attitudes, formalised and romanticised by time, which have been handed down to him from an earlier and very different war. Lacking his dead brother's gaiety of spirit, his search for death becomes a meaningless ritual, pursued not with bravado but with a kind of sullen desperation. Narcissa Benbow, his second wife, tries to help him—though she seems to be in love with the image of Bayard's dead brother rather than with Bayard himself—but she is unable to give him more than temporary relief, and eventually he does kill himself by taking up an aircraft which he knows to be unsafe.

It is sometimes said that Faulkner in this novel wholeheartedly endorses the "Sartoris" values, as exemplified above all by the dead Colonel John. This is to overlook both Miss Jenny's attitude towards the Sartoris men and those other passages in the novel in which the "Sartoris" values are seen critically and in clear perspective. Before Miss Jenny recounts the death of an earlier Bayard Sartoris, her own and Colonel John Sartoris's brother, we are told explicitly that what had actually been "a harebrained prank of two heedless and reckless boys" had become in the course of years a "finely tragical focal point" of history,[12] while the final rhetorical passage about the Sartorises, not always quoted in full, contains nicely-balanced measures of criticism and celebration:

The music went on in the dusk softly; the dusk was peopled with ghosts of glamorous and old disastrous things. And if they were just glamorous enough, there was sure to be a Sartoris in them, and then they were sure to be disastrous. Pawns. But the Player, and the game He plays. . . . He must have a name for His pawns, though. But perhaps Sartoris is the game itself —a game outmoded and played with pawns shaped too late and to an old dead pattern, and of which the Player Himself is a little wearied. For there is death in the sound of it, and a glamorous fatality, like silver pennons downrushing at sunset, or a dying fall of horns along the road to Roncevaux.[13]

This is as near as Faulkner ever comes to subscribing to the "Southern legend" in its traditional form, and even as he does so he testifies to its complete anachronism. The name of Sartoris may have about it a "glamorous fatality," but it has at the same time an undeniable, if still glamorous, futility.

In *Sartoris* Faulkner is still a minor novelist, but in the same year, 1929, he published *The Sound and the Fury*, one of the major novels of the twentieth century. It is also one of the century's most exacting novels. Faulkner makes few concessions to his readers, and some of the most sensitive among them have found the book irritating, grotesque, and even meretricious. Certainly Faulkner has come a long way from the traditional forms of the nineteenth-century novel, but the book should present no great difficulties to readers familiar with the work of James Joyce, to whom, directly or indirectly, Faulkner is much indebted. Like so much of Faulkner's work, it has to be persevered with until eye and mind become attuned to its peculiarities of structure and technique, but the perseverance will bring its reward: properly approached, the novel is capable of yielding up an extraordinary richness and of involving the reader in an immensely exciting process of imaginative re-creation.

Like *Absalom, Absalom!*, *The Sound and the Fury* is a story of "blood," of heredity and intense family relationships, the story of a great house in decay. The house of Compson, having produced a governor and a general, has something like aristocratic status in the world of Jefferson and Yoknapatawpha County, and it was a Compson ancestor who obtained from the Indians the square mile of land (Compson's Mile) which later occupied much of the centre of Jefferson. The Compsons with whom the novel deals, however, are those of the last generation, an enfeebled remnant of the old stock. They are Quentin, who commits suicide; Caddy (Candace), a sexual rebel and outcast from her home; Jason, who becomes a soulless petty-businessman; and Benjy (christened Maury), who is an idiot. The parents—Mr Compson, sententious and ineffectual, and Mrs Compson, a whining hypochondriac

—provide a domestic environment (presented vividly throughout the book in brief impressionistic vignettes) which combines readily with the effects of heredity to drive the children along their terrible paths.

The action of the book extends from the childhood of Quentin, Caddy, Jason, and Benjy—born in that order—in the late eighteen-nineties to Easter Sunday, 1928, when Caddy's unhappy daughter, called Quentin after her dead uncle, runs away from home with a man from a travelling fair. This action is not presented chronologically, however; it is, indeed, the violent disruption of the chronology which provides in this novel, as elsewhere in Faulkner's work, one of the major obstacles to a swift comprehension of its structure and meaning. What is immediately obvious is that *The Sound and the Fury* is divided into four quite separate sections: the first of these, Benjy's, is dated April 7, 1928 (Easter Saturday); the second, Quentin's, is dated June 2, 1910; the third, Jason's, is dated April 6, 1928 (Good Friday); while the fourth, told from the point of view of the omniscient author, is dated April 8, 1928 (Easter Sunday).

Benjy's section is a technical *tour de force*, one of the most famous in modern literature. Here the tale of "sound and fury" is literally "told by an idiot," and to Benjy himself it signifies little. Clearly Faulkner cannot render accurately in words the thought-processes of someone for whom words have no symbolic meaning, and what he really gives us in this section is a series of physical impressions recorded directly, without the intervention of an ordering and interpreting intelligence. It is a convention of pure objectivity, into which abstractions cannot enter, least of all the abstraction called time. For Benjy "time past" and "time present" are as one, and what happened thirty years ago is as vivid and alive as what is happening in the novel's "now."

The section opens in "time present" with Luster, Benjy's current Negro nurse, walking with him along the fence bordering the golf-course—we learn later that this course was formerly "Benjy's pasture," the last remnant of the original "Compson mile," but had been sold many years before so that Quentin could go to Harvard. Luster is searching for a quarter which will buy him admission to the travelling fair which has come to town, and throughout the section Luster's name and his frantic desire for a quarter provide a persistent *motif* by which "time present" may be readily identified. The bulk of the section, however, consists of scenes from "time past" which are recalled to Benjy's mind by what are usually fairly obvious associative transitions: getting into bed or watching the fire in the present prompts the resurgence of similar experiences from the past; the sight of Quentin on the swing with a man brings back to Benjy the re-membered sight of her mother, Caddy, in the same situation.

The alternation of roman and italic type is used to in-dicate that a shift of this kind has taken place in Benjy's rudimentary consciousness—the italicised passages do not themselves form any pattern—and once the conven-tion is grasped the section immediately appears much less complex than it does at first. Indeed, the incidents which intrude upon Benjy's consciousness derive for the most part from a few clearly-distinguishable periods in the past: early childhood, for example, especially the day on which the children's grandmother (Damuddy) dies; the day when the full extent of Benjy's idiocy is recognised and his name is changed at Mrs Compson's insistence; the day of Caddy's marriage to Herbert Head in 1910; the time when Benjy molests the passing schoolgirls and is castrated.

Where Benjy's section is all objectivity, pure sensation, Quentin's moves always in the direction of abstraction. Time, honour, virginity are the dominating themes, the ideal conceptions about which Quentin's mind revolves. Quentin's memories of the past often coincide with

Benjy's, and because of this our reading of the second section progressively illuminates the first. At the same time, one important effect of the first section has been to establish firmly, through their very simplicity, certain images—the pasture, the swing among the cedars, Caddy's "smell of trees," her wedding veil, and so on—which take on greater importance here as they become involved in the intricate convolutions of Quentin's tortured thoughts. Far from being an idiot, Quentin possesses a highly intelligent and sophisticated mind, but one which is unbalanced by his ambiguous involvement with his sister and by his obsession with time and with the Compson family honour; and we learn, in a stream-of-consciousness technique that owes much to Joyce—critics have even noted strong resemblances between Quentin and Stephen Daedalus as characters[14]—of the thoughts, impressions, memories, and images that come flooding into that mind during the last day of Quentin's life. It is not stated explicitly that Quentin commits suicide that afternoon, but the repeated references to water, to the flat-irons which Quentin purchases, and to the two notes he writes, make us gradually aware that he intends to drown himself.

This awareness inevitably adds to the intensity of the whole section, which reaches its climax in the magnificent penultimate paragraph when Quentin recalls—or possibly only imagines—his attempt to persuade his father that he had committed incest with Caddy. Quentin's passionate and frantic idealism is hopelessly shattered as it comes up against the chilling imperturbability of Mr Compson's worldly wisdom. At the beginning of the following passage, for example, Mr Compson refuses to take seriously Quentin's threat of suicide:

 . . . and he we must just stay awake and see evil done for a little while its not always and i it doesnt have to be even that long for a man of courage and he do you

consider that courage and i yes sir dont you and he
every man is the arbiter of his own virtues whether or
not you consider it courageous is of more importance
than the act itself than any act otherwise you could
not be in earnest and i you dont believe i am serious
and he i think you are too serious to give me any cause
for alarm you wouldnt have felt driven to the expedient
of telling me you have committed incest otherwise and
i i wasnt lying i wasnt lying and he you wanted to sub-
limate a piece of natural human folly into a horror and
then exorcise it with truth and i it was to isolate her out
of the loud world so that it would have to flee us of
necessity and then the sound of it would be as though
it had never been and he did you try to make her do it
and i i was afraid to i was afraid she might and then it
wouldnt have done any good but if i could tell you we
did it would have been so and then the others wouldnt
be so and then the world would roar away and he and
now this other you are not lying now either but you
are still blind to what is in yourself to that part of
general truth the sequence of natural events and their
causes which shadows every mans brow even benjys
you are not thinking of finitude you are contemplating
an apotheosis in which a temporary state of mind will
become symmetrical above the flesh and aware both of
itself and of the flesh it will not quite discard you will
not even be dead and i temporary and he you cannot
bear to think that someday it will no longer hurt you
like this now were getting at it you seem to regard it
merely as an experience that will whiten your hair over-
night so to speak without altering your appearance at
all . . .[15]

Apart from the absence of punctuation the writing itself
offers no difficulty here: the use of "and he" or "and I" to
introduce direct speech in "total recall" passages such as
this is a favourite convention of Faulkner's. The difficulty,

as so often in Faulkner, lies rather in the ideas themselves. We can say, crudely, that Quentin, obsessed with Caddy's virginity as the embodiment of Compson family honour, has conceived the idea of persuading the world that they have committed incest so that the world will withdraw from them in horror and they will live, though in Hell, eternally isolated, eternally together, his and her honour eternally intact. As Mr Compson points out, however, what Quentin is really obsessed with is time, and the inadmissible fear that his passion for Caddy and for honour will not always be sustained at its present idealistic pitch. The peculiar nature of Quentin's obsessions is made clearer in the Appendix on "The Compsons" which Faulkner first wrote for Malcolm Cowley's collection *The Portable Faulkner* and which is printed as a foreword to the Modern Library edition of *The Sound and the Fury*. Ideally this extended footnote should be read after rather than before the novel, but because it does sometimes clarify and underline what Faulkner is saying in *The Sound and the Fury* it might well be turned to earlier by any reader who finds himself in difficulties.[16]

In the *Paris Review* interview Faulkner observed that the piece on the Compsons was a fifth attempt to tell a story he had already tried to tell four times already: " 'I wrote it five separate times, trying to tell the story, to rid myself of the dream which would continue to anguish me until I did.' "[17] The third and fourth of these accounts, of course, are the last two sections of the novel, and these offer few of the difficulties of their predecessors. In the third section the character and tone of voice of Jason Compson are marvellously rendered, and Faulkner's sardonic humour, which appeared earlier in the vignettes of such characters as Deacon and Mrs Bland in the Quentin section, is here everywhere in evidence:

Blood, I says, governors and generals. It's a damn good thing we never had any kings and presidents; we'd all be down at Jackson [the State lunatic asylum] chasing butterflies.[18]

The fourth and final section of the novel is technically the most "conventional." If it also seems the most successful, that may be largely due to our sense of relief at the comparative serenity of this section, which is dominated by Dilsey, the Compson's faithful and indomitable Negro servant, after the agonising intensity of the earlier ones, and to our satisfaction at the way in which so complex a novel has been rounded out. Faulkner has said of this section, "I tried to gather the pieces together and fill in the gaps by making myself the spokesman,"[19] and it is here that the whole question of the novel's meaning arises in its acutest form.

The events of the section take place on Easter Sunday, a sermon in a Negro church occupies a prominent position, and there seem to be possible suggestions of the Resurrection in the description of Jason breaking into Quentin's empty room. To this we must add the facts of Benjy's innocence, his age (33), and Dilsey's description of him as "de Lawd's chile."[20] Christian implications of a similar kind appear in other novels of Faulkner's, but it seems clear that he uses them, for the most part, in much the same way as he uses violent action—as a tool merely, as a convenient means of working towards a final statement which may not be Christian at all, and which is very unlikely to be orthodox.[21] Faulkner's main concern in this section is apparently to establish firm images of order, stability, and trust to set over against the images of disorder, decay, selfishness, and deceit which have dominated the earlier sections. Thus, on the very last page, Benjy is outraged by Luster's action in driving the carriage to the left at the monument of the Confederate soldier, instead of to the right as customary, and is only restored to calm when the direction is reversed:

The broken flower drooped over Ben's fist and his eyes

were empty and blue and serene again as cornice and
facade flowed smoothly once more from left to right;
post and tree, window and doorway, and signboard,
each in its ordered place.[22]

Above all, we have in this section the extremely positive
presentation of Dilsey, with her great fidelity, patience,
endurance, and love. She is directly contrasted with the
neurotic Mrs Compson, whose failure to give her children
love is a primary cause of the family's disintegration, and
we see that it is Dilsey alone who attempts to give Caddy
something of that affection she so desperately needs. This
is especially important in that we become increasingly
aware that Caddy's desperation, Caddy's despair, are at
the very heart of the novel, that *The Sound and the Fury* is,
in a very real sense, Caddy's book and Caddy's tragedy—
or, as Faulkner himself insists, the tragedy of "two lost
women," of Caddy and Quentin, the mother and the
daughter.[23]

The notoriously disrupted chronology of *The Sound and
the Fury* has worried many readers, but it must be remem-
bered that Faulkner is less interested in the "story," in
the conventional sense, than in exploring the differing
reactions of different characters to the same set of
events, above all to Caddy's behaviour before and
after her marriage. Although Faulkner never takes us in-
side Caddy's mind she gradually becomes the central
figure of the book, pervading it both as a character and,
especially in the first two sections, as a set of images and
associations. Her three brothers are all obsessed with her,
each in his different but wholly selfish and self-centred
way. None of them is capable of loving her. Each wants
to impose upon her, for his own selfish purposes, a rigid
and restrictive pattern of behaviour.

It is against this rigidity that Caddy rebels, first
through her sexual freedom, later through her marriage,
but she remains permanently and painfully trapped by

the fact that her daughter is a hostage in Compson hands. Quentin herself subsequently follows, and with even greater determination, the path her mother had taken, and however worthless the partner of her escape may be it is perhaps to be taken as a sign of hope that she leaves no hostage behind. Like Caddy before her, Quentin is searching desperately for love, and through the emphasis on their search, and on the all-embracing love of Dilsey as contrasted with the lovelessness of the Compson household as a whole, we come finally to realise that it is, more than anything else, the failure of love and the triumph of selfishness and egotism that has brought about the degradation and disintegration of the house of Compson.

There is still considerable critical disagreement not only about the meaning of *The Sound and the Fury* but about its quality. About Faulkner's next novel, however, there is much less doubt and controversy, and *As I Lay Dying* is widely considered to be the most completely and unquestionably successful work that Faulkner has yet produced. It is certainly, once the basic structural scheme has been grasped, one of the simplest of Faulkner's novels. The story treats of the fierce inter-relationships between the different members of the Bundren family, who live on a poor hill-farm in Yoknapatawpha County. The "I" of the title is Addie Bundren, the mother, who exacts from Anse, her husband, a promise that when she dies he will take her to Jefferson to be buried among her own kin, and the bulk of the book is taken up with an account of the family's journey to Jefferson with Addie's increasingly malodorous coffin, and of the adventures, at once horrifying and comic, which befall them on the way. The horror and the comedy co-exist throughout in a macabre manner : which emotion gets the upper hand at any particular moment depends largely on the point of view from which the action is being presented.

The novel is built up of sixty sections of widely-varying lengths unequally divided between fifteen characters, each of whom reveals a certain segment of the action and of the family situation in terms of his own particular knowledge, intelligence, and insight—revealing at the same time, of course, a good deal about himself. Seven of the fifteen are Bundrens, the remainder are their neighbours and various people with whom they come into contact in the course of their journey. Probably the most important of these is Doctor Peabody, who sometimes acts as a kind of chorus or commentator on the action, while the most peripheral are the two druggists who react in such different ways to Dewey Dell's pregnancy. This diversification and multiplication of point of view has often been praised, but it seems at times both excessive and irritating, as when Darl is presented as clairvoyant and made to report events (such as the finishing of the coffin in the rain) at which he is not present. Richard Chase has commented on the tendency of a multiple point of view to become "simply the point of view of the omniscient author."[24]

What can be said of the technique is that it does not seriously get in the way, largely because the chronology is reasonably straightforward, and that it does give scope for some excellent passages of vernacular writing. Here, for instance, is Anse cursing the road which runs below the bluff on which the farm stands:

A-laying there, right up to my door, where every bad luck that comes and goes is bound to find it. I told Addie it wasn't any luck living on a road when it come by here, and she said, for the world like a woman, "Get up and move, then." But I told her it wasn't no luck in it, because the Lord put roads for travelling: why He laid them down flat on the earth. When He aims for something to be always a-moving, He makes it long ways, like a road or a horse or a wagon, but when He aims for something to stay put, He makes it up-and-down ways, like a tree or a man. And so he

never aimed for folks to live on a road, because which
gets there first, I says, the road or the house? Did you
ever know Him to set a road down by a house? I says.
No you never, I says, because it's always men can't
rest till they gets the house set where everybody that
passes in a wagon can spit in the doorway, keeping the
folks restless and wanting to get up and go somewheres
else when He aimed for them to stay put like a tree or
a stand of corn. Because if He'd a aimed for man to be
always a-moving and going somewheres else, wouldn't
He a put him longways on his belly, like a snake? It
stands to reason He would.[25]

This suggests not only the rich folk-humour of the novel
but also Faulkner's triumphant success, evident throughout, in the evocation and definition of character through
tone of voice. But this is an exceptionally concise and
economical book, and the passage is also related to those
central themes of the novel which are made most nearly
explicit in the one section given to Addie Bundren.

The section comes as a surprise, since Addie is already
dead, and its ideas never become wholly clear, but its
main emphasis is on the meaningless abstractness of
words as contrasted with the meaningful concreteness of
actions, on the superiority of action over speech:

And so when Cora Tull would tell me I was not a true
mother, I would think how words go straight up in a
thin line, quick and harmless, and how terribly doing
goes along the earth, clinging to it, so that after a while
the two lines are too far apart for the same person to
straddle from one to the other; and that sin and love
and fear are just sounds that people who never sinned
nor loved nor feared have for what they never had and
cannot have until they forget the words. Like Cora,
who could never even cook.[26]

Addie reveals herself as a woman of passionate individuality. She has never been able to reconcile herself to her marriage with the characterless Anse who, as the earlier quotation suggests, is the supreme embodiment of the vertical impulse, and whose invariable habit is to take refuge from action in aphorism and cliché. Unable to change Anse himself, Addie has found both solace and revenge in her relationships with her children. She loves Cash, her eldest son, and he loves her with a quiet understanding that finds expression not in words but in action, specifically in the care he devotes to building her coffin and in his patient endurance of suffering so that the journey to Jefferson need not be held up.

It was the pain of Cash's birth, however, that made Addie realise than Anse had never truly violated her selfhood, her proud "aloneness," and that the words like "love" he was so fond of using were only empty abstractions. Addie therefore rejected Anse, and when Darl was born her sense of outrage and betrayal was so great that she rejected him also. Thus Darl feels that he has no mother, and is uncertain, eventually to the point of madness, of his own individuality; he does not love Addie and tries by burning her coffin to stop the journey to Jefferson. Addie's third son, Jewel, is the result of a brief affair with Whitfield, the minister, which Addie had deliberately entered into in the hope of experiencing, through the compounded sin of committing adultery with a minister of God, a violation more complete than any she had known. Jewel and Addie have a fierce mutual love which they cannot openly express: Addie can watch over Jewel while he sleeps, but Jewel can find an outlet for his feelings only in a passionate love-hate relationship with his horse.

Darl, with his clairvoyant powers, has realised the truth about Jewel—he is always questioning him about his father and declaring that "Jewel's mother is a horse"[27] —and this is the main cause of Jewel's hatred which reveals itself so violently when Darl is taken off to the lunatic asylum at Jackson. Dewey Dell attacks Darl on the same occasion for much the same reason: he alone knows that she is pregnant and wants to go to Jefferson to buy abortion pills. Addie says she gave Anse Dewey Dell to "negative" Jewel, while she gave him the last child, Vardaman, to "replace" Jewel.[28] Vardaman has troubled critics a good deal, but since he is still a child when his mother dies his identification of her with the fish probably should be taken simply as a childish confusion.

All these relationships, centring upon the mother whose powerful personality has held the family together for so long, and still holds it even in death, are continuously explored and revealed as the story of the journey to Jefferson is told. The structure of the novel is thus simultaneously centrifugal and linear: we might compare its progression to that of a wheel on the Bundrens' wagon. The linear movement, the journey itself, is a direct and overt expression of Addie's will: she has on this one occasion forced Anse out of his shelter of words into "doing," into that "going along the earth" which he so hates. It is therefore a triumph for Addie, for the Bundrens, and for the human spirit that she is buried in Jefferson at last, and the fact that several of the Bundrens are anxious to get to Jefferson for quite other reasons (Dewey Dell to get her pills, Anse to get his teeth and a new wife) does not seriously detract from the achievement. Nor does the fact that their journey, embarked upon with such solemnity by the Bundrens themselves, may appear to outsiders grotesque, monstrous, or simply comic.

The mode of *As I Lay Dying* is primarily comic: it seems quite likely that the complex modern structure has been imposed upon a straightforward anecdote in the tradition of the "tall tales" of the frontier, and the language, while entirely original, recalls and even challenges the best vernacular writing of Mark Twain. At the same time, of course, it is, like *Huckleberry Finn*, a deeply serious novel. Terrible things happen in the course of Huck's voyage down the Mississippi to free Jim, as they do during the Bundren's journey to Jefferson to free themselves of Addie, but in both books tragedy and comedy, terror and farce, are perpetually juxtaposed and reconciled in terms of the frontier-peasant tradition of humorous realism. The horror is clearly seen and acknowledged, but it is not dwelt upon obsessively and it is balanced both by laughter and by the affirmation of positive human values.

The Bundrens may bear as a group certain resemblances to the unhappy Compson family of *The Sound and the Fury*, with Addie occupying a position something like Caddy's in the earlier book, but where the positive values at the end of that novel are represented only by Dilsey, who is outside the family, in *As I Lay Dying* they do emerge from within the family itself. Cash's gradually deepening awareness of the possibilities of human relationships is sensitively conveyed in terms of the language he uses. It is this that relieves the anguish of Darl's incarceration—as Cash says, "This world is not his world; this life his life"[29]—and it confirms our sense of the triumphant nature of the Bundrens' journey.

REFERENCES

1. Tate, *The Man of Letters in the Modern World* (1957), p. 87.
2. *A Green Bough* (*Le Rameau Vert*), p. 190.
3. Runyan, "Faulkner's Poetry," *Faulkner Studies*, III (1954), p. 24. *A Green Bough* was originally announced as *A Greening Bough*.
4. Collins, Introduction to *New Orleans Sketches* (1958), pp. 27–29.
5. *Soldiers' Pay*, p. 234 (235).
6. *M.*, p. 186.
7. *M.*, p. 329.
8. *M.*, pp. 277–81.
9. *M.*, p. 243.
10. *Sartoris*, p. 1 (1).
11. *W.W.*, p. 141.
12. *Sartoris*, p. 9 (9).
13. *Sartoris*, p. 380 (380).
14. Cp. Richard Chase, *The American Novel and its Tradition* (1958), p. 233.
15. *S.F.*, pp. 195–6 (175–6).

16. *P.F.*, pp. 737–56. It is here that we learn what happens to Caddy after the end of the novel.

17. *W.W.*, p. 130.

18. *S.F.*, p. 247 (230).

19. *W.W.*, p. 130.

20. *S.F.*, p. 333 (317).

21. Cp. *W.W.*, p. 132.

22. *S.F.*, p. 336 (321).

23. *W.W.*, p. 130.

24. Chase, *op. cit.*, p. 207.

25. *A.D.*, pp. 362 (30–1).

26. *A.D.*, p. 465 (162).

27. *A.D.*, p. 409 (86).

28. *A.D.*, p. 467 (165).

29. *A.D.*, p. 532 (248).

CHAPTER III

SANCTUARY TO *ABSALOM, ABSALOM!*

The fact that *Sanctuary* is the best known of Faulkner's books and is often read for non-literary reasons has led to its being undervalued by serious critics. Many of them have thought the book's violence excessive and its language artificial, and they have found support in Faulkner's own statement, in the introduction to the Modern Library edition, that *Sanctuary* was "a cheap idea" written entirely to make money.[1] Faulkner also tells us, however, that he revised the book extensively before publication. It seems clear that this revision was a careful and deliberate piece of work and that the novel as we have it, though not one of Faulkner's major works, is remarkably successful at its own level. It certainly contains, for instance, alongside scenes of violence and horror, some of the best of Faulkner's comic episodes: the riotous funeral of Alabama Red, the solemn gentility of the three "madams" as they tipple their gin afterwards, and the saga of Virgil Snopes and Fonzo who take rooms in Miss Reba's brothel in the belief that it is an hotel.

The abrupt juxtaposition throughout *Sanctuary* of scenes of comedy with scenes of savage violence, resulting in over-emphatic ironic effects and a generally melodramatic mode of progression, has led several critics to posit an allegorical pattern for the book. The most important of these is still that put forward by George Marion O'Donnell in 1939:

In simple terms, the pattern of the allegory is something like this: Southern Womanhood Corrupted but

Undefiled (Temple Drake), in the company of the Corrupted Tradition (Gowan Stevens, a professional Virginian), falls into the clutches of amoral Modernism (Popeye), which is itself impotent, but which with the aid of its strong ally Natural Lust ("Red") rapes Southern Womanhood unnaturally and then seduces her so satisfactorily that her corruption is total, and she becomes the tacit ally of Modernism. Meanwhile Pore White Trash (Goodwin) has been accused of the crime which he, with the aid of the Naif Faithful (Tawmmy), actually tried to prevent. The Formalized Tradition (Horace Benbow), perceiving the true state of affairs, tries vainly to defend Pore White Trash. However, Southern Womanhood is so hopelessly corrupted that she wilfully sees Pore White Trash convicted and lynched; she is then carried off by Wealth (Judge Drake) to meaningless escape in European luxury. Modernism, carrying on it from birth its own impotence and doom, submits with masochistic pleasure to its own destruction for the one crime that it has not yet committed—Revolutionary Destruction of Order (the murder of the Alabama policeman, for which the innocent Popeye is executed).[2]

In simple terms, this pattern seems reasonably accurate, but it does not reflect at all adequately the issues of justice and guilt which come to the fore at the end of the novel, and it finds no place for so important a character as Ruby Lamar, the former prostitute who is now Goodwin's wife. Ruby, with her courage, her patience, her passionate love for Goodwin, is one of the few wholly admirable characters in the novel, and it is largely by comparison with her that Temple Drake is to be judged. For all its violence, the "low-life" world of the Old Frenchman place and of the Memphis brothel—the two are connected through Ruby as well as through Popeye—provides standards of human understanding and compassion by which to measure the behaviour of the "high-life" world of Temple Drake, Gowan Stevens, and Horace Benbow. It is Benbow's tragedy that he cannot believe until it is too late that his world could possibly emerge unfavourably from the comparison.

Sanctuary is perhaps the story of Benbow even more than it is the story of Temple Drake. Benbow is the most intelligent and speculative of the characters; it is his attitudes and ideas which undergo the most revolutionary change during the course of the book; and the title of the novel may be a metaphor for the rather genteel idealism, untested by experience, which Benbow retains until it is finally shattered by the judicial condemnation and lawless lynching of the innocent Goodwin, and by his own rough treatment at the hands of the crowd. It seems more likely, however, that it is intended to suggest at once the traditional purity of Southern Womanhood (cp. Temple's name) and the privileged protection of her wealthy and powerful family to which Temple is able to escape at the end of the novel.

Benbow's obsession with one representative of Southern Womanhood, Little Belle, leads him to place all his hope at the time of Goodwin's trial in another representative, Temple Drake, and his delay in interrupting her testimony at the trial, commented on by the judge, seems an indication of his reluctance to believe that Southern Womanhood could so disastrously let him down. Temple's perjury, which sends Goodwin to his death, is of a piece with the inhumanity of Narcissa and of "high" Jefferson society as a whole, as seen especially in their treatment of Ruby. But it is also of a piece with the indifference to justice shared by that society and even by such representatives of the law as Eustace Graham, the self-seeking District Attorney, and the lawyer who knew he could not help Goodwin but still accepted the payments Ruby made with her body. Peter Lisca argues that Temple's refusal to tell the truth at the trial has been forced upon her by her family and that Judge Drake is thus as indifferent to justice as the rest.[3]

Goodwin, though innocent, is condemned by a corrupt court and lynched by a mob, representative of the "free Democratico-Protestant atmosphere of Yoknapatawpha County,"[4] whose fury is compounded with sexual envy: " 'She was some baby. Jeez. I wouldn't have used no cob'," says one of them.[5] At the end of the novel the emphasis is on the corruption of a whole society and on themes of guilt, justice, and retribution, but these are by no means as fully developed as they are in *Requiem for a Nun* (1950), a sequel to *Sanctuary* which reconsiders much of the action of the earlier novel from Temple's point of view. What emerge most powerfully from *Sanctuary*, in fact, are not the abstract patterns but the story of Popeye and Temple, asserting itself by its very violence and horror, and the vividly-created life of the Memphis brothel.

Sanctuary, despite the brilliance of individual chapters, must be considered of minor importance. It was followed, in 1932, by *Light in August*, indubitably a major work. *Light in August* is the story of a man doomed, deracinated, terribly alone, engaged in a desperate, violent, and life-long search for a place in society and a sense of his own identity. In order to tell this tragic and essentially modern story, Faulkner has applied the experience gained from his experimental novels to the composition of a work that is outwardly far more "conventional" in its structure and in its representation of social reality. The action of *Light in August* unfolds coherently and more or less chronologically, though with frequent and often extensive flashbacks, and it even has a fairly complex plot, though this falls short of absolute consistency: it is not quite clear how old Christmas is at the time of his death, for example, and there is some doubt as to whether he is captured on the Friday after the murder or on the Saturday.

The external events of the story can be summarised quite briefly. Lena Grove, a country girl from Alabama, comes to Jefferson in search of Lucas Burch, the father of her unborn child, and meets instead Byron Bunch, a meek and insignificant bachelor, who falls in love with her and takes care of her until the child is born. Lena's arrival coincides with the discovery of the murder of Miss Burden, a recluse of New England abolitionist ancestry, by a bootlegger called Joe Christmas, whom everyone has hitherto taken to be white but whom his former partner Brown (alias Lucas Burch) declares to be a Negro. Christmas is pursued as a Negro and caught in Motts-town a week later. When he is brought back to Jefferson he escapes and runs to the house of the Reverend High-tower, a disgraced minister, where he is shot to death and castrated by Percy Grimm, a fanatical officer of the National Guard. Lena Grove has meanwhile given birth to her child, the Reverend Hightower acting as midwife, and when Burch/Brown runs off once more she leaves Jefferson accompanied by the doggedly faithful Byron Bunch.

The core of the novel is the story of Joe Christmas, whose life is recounted in a long flashback occupying seven of the central chapters. Christmas, who is given his name at the orphanage in Memphis where he is placed by his crazed grandfather Doc Hines, is haunted through-out his life by the knowledge that his father may have been part-Negro. He never knows the truth of the matter, and neither do we, but he is perpetually made aware of society's inflexible requirement that a man be *either* white *or* Negro and act accordingly. Christmas looks white, and society is ready to accept him as such, but some compulsion drives him again and again to say that he is a Negro. When he is among Negroes, on the other hand, he is driven to insist that he is white, and his fate is to be un-able to find rest anywhere but to oscillate frantically be-tween black and white, achieving a sense of personal identity only in the recurrent and often deliberately provoked episodes of violence which mark his career.

Many of these episodes have an almost ritualistic aspect, and this is especially true of the beatings administered by his foster-father, McEachern. Christmas hates McEachern, but at least he acts predictably, according to a code of behaviour that is as clearly defined as it is inflexible, and to be punished by him is to be recognised as an individual. Christmas's hatred of women, which develops later into disgust, derives largely from his anger at their tendency to blur through pity or sentimentality the clear-cut patterns of crime and punishment. The crucial experience is the dietician's attempt to reward him when he expects to be punished, but Mrs McEachern's petty kindness confirms his attitude: she will not accept him as he is, but attempts always to manoeuvre him into acting conventionally. Finally, throughout their long relationship and even in her wildest sexual transports, Miss Burden never forgets that he is a Negro. It is this awareness that intensifies her sense of sinning against her Calvinistic God, and, when their physical relationship is at an end, it is her insistence that Joe choose, once and for all, the social role of Negro—by going to a college for Negroes and acting as an agent in her Northerner's scheme for uplifting the Negro race—that drives them to the final violent confrontation, when she tries to kill him, again almost ritualistically, with a Civil War pistol, and he murders her with his razor.

Ironically, the supreme act of violence by which Christmas frees himself from Miss Burden is the direct cause of his becoming finally categorised by society as a "nigger murderer," to be hunted down and disposed of according to the established rituals by which Southern society disposes of all "nigger murderers." Christmas's attempts to break free of his destiny are perpetually frustrated, and he is frequently associated in the novel with images of the circle, most explicitly at the end of Ch. 14, when he is travelling in the Negro waggon to Mottstown to give himself up:

> Looking, he can see the smoke low on the sky, beyond an imperceptible corner; he is entering it again, the street which ran for thirty years. It had been a paved street, where going should be fast. It had made a circle and he is still inside of it. Though during the last seven days he has had no paved street, yet he has travelled further than in all the thirty years before. And yet he is still inside the circle. "And yet I have been further in these seven days than in all the thirty years", he thinks. "But I have never got outside that circle. I have never broken out of the ring of what I have already done and cannot ever undo", he thinks quietly, sitting on the seat, with planted on the dashboard before him the shoes, the black shoes smelling of negro: that mark on his ankles the gauge definite and ineradicable of the black tide creeping up his legs, moving from his feet upward as death moves.[6]

Christmas wants only rest and quiet—a little earlier, feeling the freshness of the dawn, he realises with amazement: " 'That was all I wanted. . . . That didn't seem a whole lot to ask in thirty years' "[7]—but peace is the one thing that his past and his environment will not permit him. He must run always in his terrible circle, not in any sense a villain, as Faulkner is at pains to emphasise, but a man doomed, the victim of his heredity and upbringing and of society at large. The main function of the much-discussed Christ-imagery which clusters around Christmas, especially at the moment of his death, is not to make him a "Christ-figure"—an unnecessarily portentous term—but to underline his role as a sacrificial victim.

Christmas, after all, is not the bearer of the positive values of the novel, but the tragic helpless victim of "naturalistic" fiction, destroyed by forces beyond his control. The sense of resurgent hope, of endurance, of new life which emerges at the end of the novel is mainly embodied in the figure of Lena Grove. Not only does Lena both begin and end the novel, as if to frame and contain the story of Christmas, but her steady imperturbable onward linear progress through the book is in direct contrast to the other's frantic circling. Like Eula Varner of *The Hamlet*, Lena, healthy, handsome, fertile, rather stupid, is one of those "earth-mother" figures of Faulkner's who are perhaps nearer to his Negroes than to any other of his white women.

The birth of Lena's child is a focal point for the positive elements in the novel, those that are on the side of the "life" that Lena herself so abundantly possesses and represents. As an explicit image of rebirth it is an obvious counterpoise to the death of Christmas, and this is emphasised by the way in which old Mrs Hines, the grandmother of Christmas, confuses the newborn baby with the grandson she had known only as a child. That the child's birth is also related to the death of Miss Burden is emphasised by its taking place on the dead woman's plantation and by Hightower's explicit comment: " 'Poor, barren woman. To have not lived only a week longer, until luck returned to this place. Until luck and life returned to these barren and ruined acres.' "[8] For Hightower himself, who indulges the hope that the child will be named after him, the birth is the direct cause of his own re-entry into life and of his reawakened sensitivity to the beauty and fecundity of the natural world. And for Byron, who becomes the child's substitute father, the birth marks the end of his isolation, of his attempt to avoid involvement in the affairs of Jefferson and the world.

Lena, of course, is to some extent a comic character. As the world sees her she is a stock figure of rural humour, and by presenting the final episode through the eyes of the truck-driver, Faulkner forces us to see her in that light at the last. It is part of the richness of the book, however, that characters vividly presented on the realistic level nevertheless carry wider implications which contribute to the total meaning of the novel. The title itself works in this way: "light in August," according to Malcolm Cowley,[9] is a country phrase referring to Lena's pregnancy, but it carries suggestions also of the imagery of light and dark which runs throughout the book and of the moral illumination which comes finally to Christmas and, above all, to Hightower. It is Hightower who makes it clear that Lena's story is not merely comic relief to the story of Christmas: "The good stock peopling in tranquil obedience to it the good earth; from these hearty loins without hurry or haste descending mother and daughter."[10] Lena and her child represent in the novel those qualities of the natural life—fecundity, patience, endurance, trust and a simple enjoyment of experience—which are in such contrast to the narrow, insensitive, life-denying rigidity of so many of the other characters: Doc Hines, for example, McEachern, Miss Burden, Percy Grimm, and Hightower before his reawakening. There seems no doubt that in his presentation of these characters Faulkner intended a fundamental criticism of the spiritual poverty and principled inhumanity of Southern Protestantism, and the story of Hightower, the one man to emerge from rigidity into "life," is perhaps the clearest guide to the overall statement which Faulkner is making in this book.

Apart from Byron Bunch, who remains a somewhat anonymous figure, it is Hightower whose life is most profoundly changed by the advent of Christmas and Lena Grove—the two strangers who come to Jefferson and bring out, respectively, the worst and the best in its inhabitants—and we note that the chapter devoted to Hightower's history is placed almost at the end of the novel, immediately before the "framing" anecdote about Lena and Byron. Faulkner, as we have seen, has already used Hightower several times as an intelligent commentator; and in this chapter he seems to come nearest to an explicit statement of what the book is about. Hightower's obsession with the past, specifically the moment when his grandfather was shot during a Confederate cavalry raid on Yankee stores in Jefferson, has had the quality almost of an aesthete's withdrawal. It has made him immune to human feeling, remote from the wife whom he drove to suicide and from the congregation whom he should have served, and Byron Bunch's insistence that he act as mid-wife to Lena and speak to save Christmas represents a terrible violation of himself from which he recoils.

Yet Hightower does go to Lena, and does try, too late, to save Christmas; he is thus able to achieve a final realisation of his inescapable responsibility for all his actions and of his essential "oneness" with his friends, his congregation, and everyone he has known.[11] It is a vision of human interdependence and human solidarity, a reali-sation of the need for love and involvement in the fate of others, and a rejection of rigidity of spirit, of any attempt to impose an abstract pattern upon life. It is, in fact a rejection of Hightower's own past and of the lives of all those at whose hands Joe Christmas has suffered, those who have failed to respond to his needs as an individual human being and have demanded instead his conformity to patterns of behaviour befitting the social category to which they have mentally consigned him.

Pylon, Faulkner's next novel after *Light in August*, is generally agreed to be, after *Mosquitoes*, his most con-spicuous failure. The actual language of the book is highly wrought and self-consciously "artful" to an un-usual degree, but of all Faulkner's novels this is the one most lacking in clarity of conception and solidity of con-struction. It may have been his intention to create a poetic novel, dependent for its effects upon imagery, allusion, and free association, but the result is a disor-ganised and artificial book which cannot be read without a sense of strain. The "story," which has to be disentangled from a series of disconnected flashbacks, is of an uncon-

ventional "family" of fliers—Schumann, the pilot;
Laverne, his wife; Jack, the parachute jumper, who is
Laverne's openly acknowledged lover; and Jackie, the
"joint" son of the trio—who come to New Valois (New
Orleans) to take part in an air pageant which is being
staged to celebrate the opening of the new municipal airport. They are permanently poor, but in their dedication
to flying this does not normally trouble them. Now,
however, they must win the big race and get some money,
for Laverne is carrying another child. The child is Jack's,
but Schumann, knowing this, nevertheless risks his life in
the race by flying a plane which everyone knows to be
dangerous. He crashes and dies, but manages to bring the
plane down not on the crowded airport but in a lake
nearby. Laverne hands Jackie over to Schumann's father
and goes off with Jack and their unborn child.

The main centre of consciousness in the novel, though
he does not greatly illuminate either the action or the
characters—he is rather a vehicle for the imagery—is an
anonymous newspaper reporter whom Faulkner seems
deliberately to have based on Eliot's Prufrock. At first he
regards the members of the Schuman *ménage* as inhuman
monsters, not merely servants of the machine but
machines of a kind themselves, incapable of normal
human relationships. Later he comes to recognise that
they in fact possess greater potentialities for loyalty, love,
self-sacrifice, heroism, and "life" than any of the inhabitants of New Valois, an "unreal city" of meaningless
noise and movement, of anonymous crowds and corrupt,
materialistic, life-denying values. In the presentation of
New Valois Faulkner leans heavily and frankly on the
imagery of Eliot's *The Waste Land*, and Schumann's
"death by water" is apparently intended to be in some
way redemptive.

The imagery, however, seems contrived and over-
insistent, and any "statement" the book may have been
intended to enforce is fatally compromised by the sheer

obscurity of much of the writing and the absence of a clear structural principle or even of any satisfactory central intelligence and point of reference. The book seems to be composed of several disparate elements brought rather arbitrarily together and never perfectly fused. To the basic triangular situation of the story "Honor" (first published 1930, reprinted in *Dr. Martino*) Faulkner seems to have added Eliot's imagery, his own knowledge of flying and of New Orleans, and several themes taken over, no doubt unconsciously, from *Light in August*. Laverne, for instance, with her rich yellow hair, her fecundity and her indomitability, is an "earth-mother" figure, though uprooted by her involvement in the fliers' world; she is strongly reminiscent of Lena Grove, whose very name is almost an anagram of hers, as is that of Eula Varner in *The Hamlet*. The sadistic police-man who pursues Laverne vividly recalls Percy Grimm, old Dr Schumann and his wife seem derived from the Hines couple, and there are parallels to be found between the doomed life and sacrificial death of Joe Christmas and the similar fate of Schumann, a man possessed by flying, one of those who fly not for profit or for pleasure but "because they have got to do it, like some women have got to be whores. They can't help themselves."[12]

This dependence on the thematic patterns of *Light in August* hints at a failure of conception which is, in any case, obvious throughout the novel. In England, *Pylon* has been one of the most frequently reprinted of Faulkner's books, perhaps because of its treatment of sexual themes, but it is impossible to regard it as an artistic success, even of a minor kind. Certainly it is dwarfed by its great predecessor, *Light in August*, and by its even greater successor, *Absalom, Absalom!*

Absalom, Absalom! is Faulkner's most impressive achievement, a work of technical virtuosity and moral anguish on a scale not seen in American literature since Henry James's *The Wings of the Dove*. Some critics have considered the structural complexity of *Absalom, Absalom!* to be a mere act of perversity on Faulkner's part. It is in fact fundamental to the whole meaning of the book, but there is no doubt that it often dismays readers coming to *Absalom, Absalom!* for the first time. The language of the opening chapters is the most difficult of any in the novel: grandiose, intricate, convoluted, often unsyntactical, almost Elizabethan in its complexity and its splendour. The atmosphere is dark, violent, melo-dramatic. The action seems confused, full of obscure hints of future catastrophes and enigmatic glimpses into a mysterious past, and it is only gradually that a firm pattern begins to emerge. Once the pattern has emerged, however, it is never lost sight of—though always shifting, always appearing in new lights, always being modified—and it grows steadily richer in its implications, more com-pelling in its power over our imaginations. This is true above all of the last pages when the fall of the house of Sutpen is revealed; for it is here that the organisation of the novel brings to bear the whole weight of the tragedy upon Quentin Compson, the suicide of *The Sound and the Fury* and the chief medium through whom the story of *Absalom, Absalom!* is told.

Quentin is the novel's "medium" in a very special sense, for it is through him that we hear the voices of men and women absent and dead, and it is in his imagination, and in the precisely-attuned imagination of his Harvard room-mate Shreve, that the final poetic reconstruction of the story takes place. The reconstruction is "poetic" be-cause we are never presented, in this extraordinary book, with the "truth" about Thomas Sutpen. The bare facts of Sutpen's story, of course, are established in the opening pages, together with the main images which are to be associated with him throughout the book:

Out of quiet thunderclap he would abrupt (man-horse-demon) upon a scene peaceful and decorous as a

schoolprize water color, faint sulphur-reek still in hair
clothes and beard, with grouped behind him his band
of wild niggers like beasts half tamed to walk upright
like men, in attitudes wild and reposed, and manacled
among them the French architect with his air grim,
haggard, and tatter-ran. Immobile, bearded and hand
palm-lifted the horseman sat; behind him the wild
blacks and the captive architect huddled quietly, carrying in bloodless paradox the shovels and picks and
axes of peaceful conquest. Then in the long unamaze
Quentin seemed to watch them overrun suddenly the
hundred square miles of tranquil and astonished earth
and drag house and formal gardens violently out of the
soundless Nothing and clap them down like cards upon
a table beneath the up-palm immobile and pontific,
creating the Sutpen's Hundred, the *Be Sutpen's Hundred*
like the oldentime *Be Light*.[13]

We know from the start that Sutpen came to Jefferson,
apparently out of nowhere, one June Sunday in 1833 and
set about creating a great plantation out of the hundred
square miles of jungle (Sutpen's Hundred) he had bought
from the Indians; that in 1838 he married Ellen Coldfield, daughter of a respected local merchant; that in
1865 Sutpen's son Henry killed his half-brother Charles
Bon to prevent him from marrying their sister Judith;
and that in 1869 Sutpen himself was killed by Wash
Jones, a poor-white whose daughter (Milly) Sutpen had
seduced. These facts are never in doubt: what is always
in doubt, however, and always open to interpretation or
conjecture, is the inner meaning of these observable
events and the whole intricate sequence of cause and
effect which links them to one another.

We are given in the novel three different interpretations of these events, of the whole Sutpen story; that of
Rosa Coldfield, Ellen's much younger sister, to whom the
ageing Sutpen, returned after the four heroic years of the

Civil War to a plantation and a family in ruins, once pro-
posed a marriage that would be conditional on her
ability to produce the son and heir he needed; that of Mr
Compson, father of Quentin, son of the General Compson
who had been Sutpen's only friend; and, finally, that of
Quentin himself as he sits with the Canadian Shreve
McConnon in their icy room at Harvard a few months
before committing the act of suicide we have already
learned of from *The Sound and the Fury*. Rosa's story, which
occupies most of Ch. I and the whole of Ch. v, is a tale of
Gothic horror, an essay in demonology, with Sutpen
himself cast in the role of Beelzebub. Mr Compson's
version, occupying Chs. II–IV, is more objective than
Rosa's, and much saner, but we come to realise that it
goes too far in the opposite direction; it is too balanced,
too self-consciously rational, to take the full measure of
Sutpen's obsession, and Mr Compson himself realises that
his account of Charles Bon's death seems to leave something unexplained.

The final chapters of the novel (VI–IX) are taken up
with the attempt of Quentin and Shreve to assemble all
the extraordinary events and characters of the Sutpen
story and make sense out of them. Quentin, in particular,
is like a detective of genius, collecting all the available
evidence, and then, with the aid of his more matter-of-fact
assistant, imaginatively reconstructing what "must" have
been the course of events and the pattern of motivation.
Because of the imaginative sympathy, amounting in Ch.
VIII to a sense of actual identification, which Quentin and
Shreve feel for the dead Henry and Charles, their version
achieves a "poetic truth" of a wholly convincing kind.
It is not, however, to be taken as a factually accurate
account—despite the fact that it is based on fuller infor-
mation than the two earlier ones and is obviously much
nearer the "truth"—for to do so would be to miss an
important aspect of the book's richness.

The three accounts do not simply fill out the story and

clothe it with meaning, they brilliantly illuminate the personalities of the respective story-tellers. Thus Rosa's account concentrates on Sutpen's relations with his womankind, Mr Compson's on Sutpen's relationship to the society of Jefferson and of the South generally, Quentin-Shreve's on the relationships between Sutpen, Charles, Henry, and Judith; and what emerges so vividly from these different versions is Rosa's frustrated bitterness, Mr Compson's ineffectual cynicism, and the eager romantic idealism of the two young men, qualified on Quentin's part by his personal involvement with the South and with that theme of incest which is of such importance in *The Sound and the Fury* and in the Biblical story of Absalom in II Sam. XIII–XIX.

At one level, then, *Absalom, Absalom!* is a study of the characters of Rosa, Mr Compson, and Quentin, as revealed by their different reactions to the same set of events; and, to this extent, it is in the same experimental line as *The Sound and the Fury* and *As I Lay Dying*. *Absalom, Absalom!* differs from these earlier books, however, in several important ways. The different reflexions or interpretations of the central story, instead of being separated out into distinct sections, are intimately interwoven within an extremely complex and carefully-articulated novel structure. The different versions constantly overlap, contradict, confirm, and revalue each other, and it is by this means that Faulkner achieves those audacious ambiguities, juxtapositions, and effects of delayed revelation which give the novel its extraordinary qualities of moral complexity and narrative suspense.

The structural complexity of *Absalom, Absalom!*, far from being an arbitrary imposition, thus embodies the very meaning of the work. Not only does the "story" exist solely in terms of its various reflexions, the whole novel is "about" the inextricable confusion of fact and fiction, of observation and interpretation, involved in any account of human experience. Or we might say that it is a demonstration of the difficulties of writing history, of the impossibility of defining "Truth," of the evolution of a myth, or even of the way in which a simple idea may grow in the hands of an artist into a thing of beauty and grandeur—as perhaps the short story "Wash" of 1934, which contains the germ of *Absalom, Absalom!*, evolved gradually in Faulkner's mind into the major novel of 1936.

It is useful, up to a point, to think of *Absalom, Absalom!* as a demonstration of this kind, but there is certainly nothing about it of a coldly-undertaken literary exercise. It bears, on the contrary, all the marks of having been written out of an intense inner compulsion. When Shreve asks Quentin why he hates the South, his agonised reply ends the novel on a note of personal nightmare which we feel must be partly Faulkner's own:

" 'I dont hate it', Quentin said, quickly, at once, immediately; 'I dont hate it', he said. *I dont hate it* he thought, panting in the cold air, the iron New England dark; *I dont. I dont! I dont hate it! I dont hate it!*"[14]

For Quentin, as for Faulkner, the story of Sutpen is in some sense an image of that South of which he is himself inescapably a part. In historical terms, Sutpen is a latecomer to the ranks of Southern gentlemen, but his achievement of that rank in a single generation is only a violent condensation of a process which in most families went on over several generations, and by the magnificence of his house and his outstanding bravery in the Civil War Sutpen proves himself a worthy representative of his new class. For Wash Jones, in the story "Wash," Sutpen is the supreme embodiment of all that is best in the South, but what Wash comes to realise is that the South at its best cannot bring itself to recognise even the simplest human need of its inferiors, the need to be recognised as human.

The point of view in the story is that of Wash rather

than of Sutpen, and the point about Sutpen's lack of human feeling is quickly and economically made, but in the novel we are at first stunned by the sheer audacity and splendour of Sutpen's design and it is only gradually that we become aware of its fatal flaw. Sutpen himself, in his terrifying innocence, seems never to have become aware of it:

> " 'You see, [he explains to General Compson] I had a design in my mind. Whether it was a good or a bad design is beside the point; the question is, Where did I make the mistake in it, what did I do or misdo in it, whom or what injure by it to the extent which this would indicate...' "15

Sutpen's "mistake," of course, is inherent in the design itself, in the monstrosity of its attempt to make human flesh and blood conform to the rigid contours of an abstract idea. His failure as a man lies in his refusal to regard even his own family as other than the instruments of his design. His failure as a Southerner lies in his refusal to regard the Negro as a human being.

The distinction is not wholly valid, of course, for the two themes in the novel are closely intertwined. Thus the tragic event at the heart of the novel, that shooting of Charles by Henry to which Quentin's tortured imagination again and again returns, is the direct outcome of Sutpen's refusal to acknowledge Charles as his son; and this refusal is due entirely, or so we gather, to the same taint of Negro blood as had caused him to repudiate Charles's mother. Since Charles repeatedly makes it clear that he would be satisfied with the least sign of recognition, the barest acknowledgment of his human identity, Sutpen's refusal becomes an apt image of the South's tragic failure to acknowledge and accommodate the minimal human needs of the Negro.

In the pattern of the novel, Sutpen's denial of Charles's

unspoken appeal harks back to the incident in Sutpen's own youth which originally prompted the conception of his grand design—the occasion, described in Ch. vii, when the young Sutpen, a poor-white fresh from the back-country, was turned away from the door of the great house by a liveried Negro footman without being given a chance to deliver his message. This scene becomes what Sutpen himself calls the "boy-symbol"[16] which the whole of his design is intended to vindicate. By a tragic irony, however, the "boy-symbol" reappears again and again in the novel with Sutpen, in the name of his design, arbitrarily refusing to hear the human appeals of others—of Wash Jones and his daughter, of Henry, and, above all, of Charles.

Looked at in yet another way, Sutpen's story is an extended example of that theme of rigidity which Faulkner earlier explored, particularly in terms of religious belief, in *Light in August*, and the fate of Joe Christmas in that novel is recalled here by the story of Valery Bon, son of Charles and the octoroon, who violently flaunts his Negro blood in a similar attempt to gain recognition for himself as a human being. Like Christmas, however, he fails in his attempt: even to Judith and Clytie, who love him after their fashion, he is not Valery Bon but "Negro," as the sleeping arrangements made for him clearly show. All that Valery Bon does do is produce a son, the idiot Jim Bond, who is left at the end of the novel to haunt Quentin with his howls and to represent, like Benjy in *The Sound and the Fury*, the final degradation of his line.

REFERENCES

1. *S.*, p. v.
2. O'Donnell, "Faulkner's Mythology," in *T.D.C.*, pp. 56–57.
3. Lisca, "Some New Light on Faulkner's *Sanctuary*," *Faulkner Studies*, ii (1953), pp. 5–9.

4. *S.*, p. 151.
5. *S.*, p. 352.
6. *L.A.*, p. 321 (321).
7. *L.A.*, p. 313 (313).
8. *L.A.*, p. 385 (385).
9. *P.F.*, p. 652.
10. *L.A.*, p. 384 (384).

11. *L.A.*, pp. 465–6 (465–6).
12. *Pylon*, p. 175 (213).
13. *A.A.*, pp. 8–9 (8–9).
14. *A.A.*, p. 378 (378).
15. *A.A.*, p. 263 (263).
16. *A.A.*, p. 261 (261).

CHAPTER IV

SHORT STORIES AND EPISODIC NOVELS

Absalom, Absalom!, Faulkner's greatest novel, closes a chapter in his career. It marks at once the culmination and the conclusion of that astonishing seven-year period between 1929 and 1936 when Faulkner published, in addition to a book of poems and two important collections of short stories, four novels now generally acknowledged to be of major stature—*The Sound and the Fury, As I Lay Dying, Light in August,* and *Absalom, Absalom!*—and three minor novels, *Sartoris, Sanctuary,* and *Pylon,* about which critical opinion is still divided.

Nothing Faulkner has written since measures up to the best work of this, his greatest and most richly creative period. Just as his earlier work, including the novels *Soldiers' Pay* and *Mosquitoes*, was marred by preciosity and self-conscious aestheticism, so much of his later work suffers from self-consciousness of a different kind: *Intruder in the Dust, Requiem for a Nun,* and *A Fable,* for example, the "committed" novels of the post-war years, are all patterned in accordance with a deliberate and preconceived intention to enforce some kind of moral or social statement. The other novels since *Absalom, Absalom!* differ greatly in kind and in quality, but are all characterised by the absence of that structural continuity normally expected of a novel. Although in *Absalom, Absalom!* Faulkner triumphantly refuted those critics who claimed that he was incapable of sustained architectural effects, much of his subsequent work suggests that, as a general rule, the critics may have been very nearly right. None of these episodic novels is entirely successful as a whole, but they do contain some of Faulkner's finest writing—the "Old Man" section of *The Wild Palms*, for instance, and the chapters "The Bear" and "Pantaloon in Black" in *Go Down, Moses*—and what is particularly interesting is the close relationship which exists between them and Faulkner's short stories. *The Unvanquished* and *Go Down, Moses*, for example, have a sufficiently clear internal unity to be considered as novels, but they are none the less made up of separate stories, most of them previously published elsewhere.

Faulkner has so far published something like seventy-five short stories, beginning in 1930 with "A Rose for Emily," still the most famous of them all. "A Rose for Emily" and twelve other stories were included in *These 13* (1931), seven of them appearing there for the first time; and a second collection; *Dr. Martino and Other Stories* (1934), contained fourteen stories, all but two of which had previously been published in magazines. The *Collected Stories* (1950) contains forty-two stories, and most of the others are included, sometimes after considerable revision, in *The Unvanquished, Knight's Gambit* (1949), *Go Down, Moses,* or incorporated into the structure of one of the novels of the "Snopes" trilogy, *The Hamlet* (1940), *The Town* (1957), and *The Mansion* (1959). Only a very few remain uncollected, and, with the possible exception of those in *Knight's Gambit*, very few of those which have been collected seem unworthy of republication. The general level of Faulkner's short stories is high, and the best of them are unquestionably among the great short stories of this century.

The stories are thus to be regarded as important in their own right, not merely as off-shoots of the novels—the process of creation, indeed, seems almost always to have worked the other way, as with the growth of "Wash" into *Absalom, Absalom!* and of "Honor" into *Pylon*—or as complementary background material to the "Yoknapatawpha legend." At the same time, it is part of the importance of the stories that they form with the novels a clearly-unified body of work, linked not only by common themes and moral preoccupations but by the recurrence of characters and settings and, even, now and again, by actual narrative continuity—such as exists, for instance, between *Sartoris* and "There Was A Queen," and between "Barn Burning" and *The Hamlet*. Episodes, characters and scenes central to one work appear on the periphery of another, bringing with them a set of implications which extend the meaning of that second story or novel in which they play only a minor part; and it is this process, as much as anything else, which makes us aware of the potential richness and variety of the apparently restricted geographical and social area of Yoknapatawpha County.

Faulkner's short stories extend over a much wider range of characters and settings than do his novels: but, though some of the stories of the First World War, notably "Turnabout" and "All the Dead Pilots," are of high quality, Faulkner's best short stories are nearly all concerned with the characters and themes of Yoknapatawpha County. In *These 13*, for example, Faulkner's earliest and best collection of stories, "Red Leaves" and "A Justice" are both tales of the Indians who were in Yoknapatawpha County before the white man, "That Evening Sun" is peopled by the Compson household, while "A Rose for Emily" and "Dry September" are both set in Jefferson.

These are five of Faulkner's finest stories. "Red Leaves" is the story of the Negro body-slave to an Indian chief who runs away when his master dies but is eventually hunted down and brought back to share the chief's grave: here the theme of the hunt, so important in Faulkner, is applied for the first time to the pursuit of a human being. "A Justice" is one version of the origins of Sam Fathers, told by Sam himself to Quentin Compson as a boy. Basically a "tall tale," the convention is skilfully manipulated to bring out the specifically Indian cunning and intelligence of Doom, the Indian chief; and although the story itself is extremely funny, our response to it is qualified by an awareness of its implications for Sam himself as a man of mixed Negro and Indian blood. The story is in the tradition of American South-Western humour, but Faulkner does not choose to employ here the colloquial speech Mark Twain recreated so brilliantly in *Huckleberry Finn*: it does appear, however, and with great success, in stories like "Fool About a Horse" and the original version of "Spotted Horses."[1]

"That Evening Sun," "A Rose for Emily," and "Dry September," roughly similar in period and setting, are also alike in that the action of each of them takes place on the very edge of scenes of violence and horror which we do not actually witness. In "That Evening Sun," Nancy, the Compson's Negro laundress, attempts to stave off a little longer the expected murderous assault of her husband, Jesus, by gathering the Compson children around her; and the terror of the story increases in direct proportion to our growing realisation that the children do not understand Nancy's plight and will do nothing to abet her scheme. The selfishness of Mrs Compson and the ineffectiveness of Mr Compson have forced Nancy to rely upon an uncomprehending Quentin, whose "innocent eye" makes him the ideal narrator, an automatically recalcitrant Jason, and a Caddy whose half-awareness of the situation gives a brutal pointedness to her questions and observations.

"A Rose for Emily," though set in Jefferson, stands somewhat apart from the rest of Faulkner's stories as an exercise in the macabre tale with a shock ending. As such it could hardly be surpassed, and its high reputation is amply deserved. To over-emphasise the importance of "A Rose for Emily," however, is to give a false impression of Faulkner's stories as a group, and the concentration of critics upon this one story has sometimes led them to ignore others of comparable power and richness. "Dry September," for example, has received less attention than it deserves, for it is a remarkable story in which a rich social background and a group of fully-realised characters are firmly established, and a pattern of tragic action completed, with great economy and power.

The story of "Dry September" concerns the lynching of a Negro for an attack on a white woman which, it becomes clear to us, never in fact took place. With great technical skill, Faulkner alternates the violent action of the first, third, and fifth sections, centring upon McLendon, the leader of the lynching-party, with the quiet, almost discursive mood of the second and fourth sections. These tell the story of Minnie Cooper, whom the Negro is said to have attacked, and reveal a character driven to madness, like Emily Grierson of "A Rose for Emily," by frustration and isolation. The heat and drought suggested by the title are continually evoked throughout the story, not only as "atmosphere" but as active agents, in that they offer a natural provocation to violence. We also become gradually aware that they have a certain symbolic importance, never insisted upon but always present, in their relation to the acts of passionate unreason and the lives of sterile unreality with which the story deals.

Most of Faulkner's work has been in the more extended forms of fiction. His natural inclination seems to lead him towards a certain repetitiousness of words, scenes and situations, and towards effects of accretion rather than of concentration. Yet he is also a great writer of short stories, and the technical restrictions of the short story form seem, paradoxically, to release his powers rather than confine them. Faulkner is perhaps more consistently at his best in the short stories than he is in the novels, and in his most successful stories we find an intensity of effect, allied with directness of style and firmness of thematic treatment, which puts them indisputably among his greatest achievements. In "Barn Burning," for example, first published in *Harper's* in June 1939, reprinted in the *Collected Stories*, the story is told in strict chronological order and in a style of great clarity, and offers no difficulty to the reader. Yet it is, for all its apparent simplicity, a story of considerable structural sophistication and of great moral and emotional complexity.

"Barn Burning" centres upon the experience of Colonel Sartoris Snopes, younger son of Ab, the original horse-stealing Snopes, and upon the terrible conflict set up within him by his emotional attachment to his father and his moral revulsion from the acts of violence and arson his father commits. The great richness of the story derives very largely from the fact that the action is seen from the point of view of the boy himself. This use of a young and innocent witness is a favourite device of Faulkner's (cp. "That Evening Sun" and "Shingles for the Lord"), and its effect here is not to limit the meaning of the story, nor the depth of the characterisation, but actually to expand them in a quite remarkable way. The world's contempt for Ab Snopes is exactly inverted by the boy, to whom he is far and away the most important thing in the universe, so that Ab, a casually-sketched caricature elsewhere in Faulkner's work, becomes for once a solid and impressive presence. To the boy, and hence to us, Ab is a gigantic figure, and it is this that makes the boy's emotional compulsions at once so powerful and so terrifying.

It is characteristic of the connexion between Faulkner's short stories and his novels, and of the close inter-relationship of all Faulkner's work, that several echoes of "Barn Burning" should occur elsewhere. The most important of these is the episode near the beginning of *The Hamlet* when, shortly after Jody Varner has become Ab Snopes's new landlord, Ratliff, the sewing-machine agent, arrives and recounts the story of "Barn Burning." As Ratliff tells it, however, it becomes simply a humorous "tall tale" with the agony of Colonel Sartoris Snopes omitted, and it is interesting to compare the two versions to see how a change in point of view has turned tragedy into comedy. Ab Snopes reappears many times in Faulkner's work, but he is never again so vividly evoked: there seems no very close relationship, for example, between the Ab Snopes of "Barn Burning" and the Ab Snopes of *The Unvanquished* (1938), Faulkner's next book after *Absalom, Absalom!*

The Unvanquished is essentially a sequence of stories, all but the last previously published in magazines between September 1934 and December 1936 and reprinted here with, for the most part, only minor revisions. There can be no doubt, however, that the book does have sufficient continuity of characters, situations and themes to be considered a novel: the pattern of motivation is not always adequately worked out, and the mood of the last story differs too abruptly from that of its predecessors, but for all practical purposes this is one of the loosely-constructed, episodic novels typical of this phase of Faulkner's career. For the reader coming to Faulkner's work for the first time *The Unvanquished* is probably as good a place as any to start. It is the least difficult of his novels, and if it gives little inkling of his greatness it gives ample proof of his readability. More important, the book does touch, however lightly, on some of the major themes which run through the whole of Faulkner's work, and it does contain some of his most persistently recurrent characters, so that it gives the newcomer an immediate foothold in the world of Yoknapatawpha County. It is similar in this way to *Sartoris*, a book to which it is intimately related at many points, but it concerns itself much more exclusively with the business of being a Sartoris and less with the world at large.

The various stories which go to make up the novel are told from the point of view of young Bayard Sartoris—whom we have met previously as Old Bayard, the banker, of *Sartoris*—and in most of them he is himself a participant. Much of the material is based on the tales of Colonel Sartoris put into the mouth of Will Falls in

Sartoris, but they take on greater dramatic intensity from being told in the first person: although *The Unvanquished* is a less interesting and less important novel than *Sartoris*, there can be no doubt that it is the more exciting of the two. This excitement, however, is superficial, subsisting as it does almost entirely in the narrative pace, and the book does not emerge well from a second reading. The action takes place during and immediately after the Civil War, and most of the stories are romantic evocations of the heroism and ingenuity of Confederate colonels and grandmothers displayed at the expense of sometimes courteous but always gullible Yankees. The exceptions are "Vendée" and the final story, "An Odor of Verbena." "Vendée" is a violent and somewhat repulsive story in which young Bayard and his Negro companion pursue and eventually revenge themselves upon their grandmother's murderer with a vindictiveness and savagery almost equal to his own. It seems just possible that Faulkner had this story in mind in portraying the more altruistic but no less macabre enterprise of young Chick Mallison and his Negro companion in *Intruder in the Dust*.

The theme of "Vendée," however, is inverted within *The Unvanquished* in the story "An Odor of Verbena": this story, indeed, inverts or revalues so many of the previous stories that it seems scarcely to belong within the covers of the same book. Colonel Sartoris has been shot down in the street by Redmond—a situation directly recalling, like so many others in this book, the stories of Faulkner's own great-grandfather—but Bayard, called upon to revenge him, refuses to do so. Instead, he goes to Redmond's office unarmed. Redmond fires twice, aiming past him, and then leaves town. Outside, the men of his father's troop wait for Bayard, bewildered, admiring his courage, yet scarcely comprehending his purpose. It is their leader, however, who sees that Bayard may be right, that perhaps there had been enough killing in the

Sartoris family already, and we think back to Bayard's own picture of his father earlier in the story:

Then I stood again like soldiers stand, gazing at eye level above his head while he sat half-turned from the table, a little paunchy now though not much, a little grizzled too in the hair though his beard was as strong as ever, with that spurious forensic air of lawyers and the intolerant eyes which in the last two years had acquired that transparent film which the eyes of carnivorous animals have and from behind which they look at a world which no ruminant ever sees, perhaps dares to see, which I have seen before on the eyes of men who have killed too much, who have killed so much that never again as long as they live will they ever be alone.[2]

The story may perhaps be regarded as Faulkner's final statement on the Sartoris legend, and it is clear evidence that despite the relaxed romanticising of much of *The Unvanquished* he is fully aware of the limitations of the Sartoris code, and of that Southern aptness for violent action to which it is so intimately related. Bayard Sartoris's deliberate choice of non-violence not only revalues the earlier stories in *The Unvanquished* but looks forward to later celebrations of non-violence in *Intruder in the Dust* and *A Fable*.

Faulkner's next book, *The Wild Palms* (1939), stands rather apart from the rest of his work, but it falls quite aptly into place in a chapter which is largely concerned with the relationships between Faulkner's short fiction and his novels. *The Wild Palms*, the product of a rather curious technical experiment on Faulkner's part, is perhaps best described as a double novel with two plots, consisting as it does of two stories—the title story and one called "Old Man"—which alternate, chapter by chapter, throughout the book. "Wild Palms" is the story of Harry Wilbourne, a young doctor, and Charlotte Rittenmeyer,

a married woman with two children, who give up everything for love, challenging society and "respectability" at
every step. Eventually they meet with the disaster that
we recognise as inevitable, with Harry sentenced to fifty
years' imprisonment for performing the unsuccessful
abortion which brings about Charlotte's death. "Old
Man" is the story of a convict who is sent out in a skiff at
the height of a terrible Mississippi flood to rescue a
woman from a tree and a man from the roof of a cottonhouse. He finds the woman, who is eight months pregnant, but before he can find the man the floodwaters
whirl him away through a series of violent adventures,
involving tidal waves, fights with alligators, and the
birth of the woman's child on a snake-infested Indian
mound, until many weeks later he returns to his point of
departure and surrenders himself with the words,
" 'Yonder's your boat, and here's the woman. But I
never did find that bastard on the cottonhouse.' "[3]

There is no direct relationship between the two stories,
except that Harry is sentenced to the same prison as the
tall convict of "Old Man," and they do not even co-exist
in time: "Old Man" is dated 1927, the action of "Wild
Palms" takes place mostly in 1937. Because of this, many
critics have considered the experiment of continual juxtaposition to be arbitrary and unsuccessful. Editions of the
book have been published with the two stories printed
separately—in tandem instead of in parallel—and a
similar process of reconstruction goes on in our minds as
we read the book in its original form. There is no doubt,
however, that by alternating the two stories Faulkner
forces us to read each in terms of the other, and, looking
back, we realise that there are parallels and contrasts between the two which in some degree extend and modify
the meaning of both. Faulkner's idea does have its effect,
but it is one which we become aware of after we have
finished the book rather than while we are actually reading it.

Nearly everyone who reads the book finds the story of the tall convict in "Old Man" much the more impressive of the two: Malcolm Cowley, printing it as a separate story in *The Portable Faulkner*, calls it "the only other story of the Mississippi that can be set beside *Huckleberry Finn* without shrivelling under the comparison."[4] "Old Man" has something of the essential simplicity of theme and, to some extent, of language which distinguishes Hemingway's short novel *The Old Man and the Sea*, though it is without the later book's symbolic portentousness. For Faulkner, however, "Wild Palms" is the core of the book, as his comments in the *Paris Review* interview make clear:

That was one story—the story of Charlotte Rittenmeyer and Harry Wilbourne, who sacrificed everything for love, and then lost that. I did not know it would be two separate stories until after I had started the book. When I reached the end of what is now the first section of *The Wild Palms*, I realised suddenly that something was missing, it needed emphasis, something to lift it like counterpoint in music. So I wrote on the "Old Man" story until "The Wild Palms" story rose back to pitch. Then I stopped the "Old Man" story at what is now its first section, and took up "The Wild Palms" story until it began again to sag. Then I raised it to pitch again with another section of its antithesis, which is the story of a man who got his love and spent the rest of the book fleeing from it, even to the extent of voluntarily going back to jail where he would be safe. They are only two stories by chance, perhaps necessity. The story is that of Charlotte and Wilbourne.[5]

This explanation corresponds fairly closely to our actual experience when reading the book, but it is obviously over-simplified. Although the main motivation of Harry and Charlotte may have been the power of their love, which involved a continual rejection of society, the motivation of the convict seems to be not so much the flight from love of which Faulkner speaks as the desire to escape from the chaos of the flood to the ordered, familiar society of the prison. Where Faulkner's account of the book is particularly valuable is in directing our attention away from the simple, easily-admired figure of the convict to the more complex, less obviously admirable figures of Harry and Charlotte. As Olga Vickery points out,[6] they are deeper and more sensitive characters than the convict, and theirs is a tragic story, where his, though heroic, is fundamentally comic, much as the story of the Bundrens in *As I Lay Dying* is fundamentally comic without ceasing to be admirable.

It is difficult to be entirely happy about the "Wild Palms" story, however. It seems doubtful whether Faulkner has fully plumbed the depths of the situation, and the impression grows that the story and the characters have been manipulated in order to conform to a preconceived pattern. The irresistible power which love —the abstract idea as much as the actual relationship— holds over Harry and Charlotte drives them to such extremes of revolt against society, against other human relationships (as in their casting-off of Charlotte's family and of McCord), and finally against nature (the abortion), that their story becomes an image of that absolute shared isolation which fascinates such characters as Quentin Compson, and which Harry himself describes as *"the passionate idea of two damned and doomed and isolated forever against the world and God and the irrevocable."*[7]

This is a plainer statement of the theme than we find in *The Sound and the Fury* or anywhere else in Faulkner, just as later in the book we find particularly straightforward statements of the themes of time and virginity.[8] There is also a particularly moving and clear expression of Faulkner's humanism. Harry, in prison after his sentence, rejects suicide, choosing to live into a hopeless future in order that the memory of what he and Charlotte achieved may survive a little longer, and the "Wild Palms" story closes with his simple affirmation in the very teeth of tragedy: "*between grief and nothing I will take grief.*"[9]

Although *The Wild Palms* was highly praised on its first appearance, it has received relatively little attention in recent years. *Go Down, Moses* (1942), on the other hand, has become increasingly a focal point of Faulkner criticism. This is perhaps not so much because of the book's inherent quality, though that is undoubtedly high, as because of its importance in the development of Faulkner's social and moral ideas. "The Bear," in particular, has been discussed and analysed in detail by a number of critics, and the attraction it seems to possess for anthologists has made it one of Faulkner's best-known pieces. The version of "The Bear" printed in *Go Down, Moses* differs considerably from the version previously printed in the *Saturday Evening Post*:[10] it has been revised throughout and an entire new section has been added, the now famous fourth section, in which Ike McCaslin, the central figure both in the story and in *Go Down, Moses* as a whole, tries to explain to his cousin McCaslin ("Cass") Edmonds why he has repudiated his claim to the land which has come to him by direct inheritance from his grandfather Carothers McCaslin, who is Cass's great-grandfather on his mother's side.

The fourth section of "The Bear" is crucial to our understanding of *Go Down, Moses* as a novel, rather than as the collection of separate stories it appears to be at first sight, but it has perhaps been thrust a little arbitrarily into the story of the hunt for "Old Ben," the great bear, recounted in sections I, II, III, and V. This story deals with the pursuit of a real beast who becomes increasingly, as in *Moby-Dick* and Hemingway's *The Old Man and the Sea*, a magical and symbolic beast. The narrative moves forward by a series of steps corresponding to Ike's progressive initiation, already begun in "The Old People," into the ways of the wilderness. Under the tutelage of Sam

Fathers, son of an Indian chief and a Negro slave, he first hears the bear, then becomes aware that the bear has come to look at him; later he goes out with gun, watch, and compass to look at the bear: but only when he casts aside all mechanical trappings and goes out absolutely alone does the bear finally appear to him. At this point a new progression begins with the introduction of Lion, the dog of immense power and ferocity, and the gradual gathering of spectators until the day when Ben is finally killed. Ben, however, has become a symbol of the wilderness and of the ideas associated with the wilderness in Faulkner's mind, ideas of freedom, courage, fecundity, and natural wisdom; and his death is followed by the death of Sam Fathers, and by the destruction at the hands of a lumber company of that section of the wilderness over which Ben presided.

It is now unfashionable to accept Malcolm Cowley's suggestion that section IV can be skipped and the remaining sections of "The Bear" read consecutively as a relatively straightforward tale of hunting,[11] but the suggestion finds support in Faulkner's own statement that section IV belongs not to the story proper but to the novel, and that it should have been omitted when the version of "The Bear" in Go Down, Moses was subsequently reprinted as an anthology piece.[12] Faulkner himself has included "The Bear," without the fourth section, in Big Woods (1953), a collection of stories of hunting and the wilderness which also reprints "The Old People" from Go Down, Moses, as well as a revised version of "Delta Autumn."

Big Woods is an unsatisfactory volume. Its central theme, the progressive destruction of the wilderness, seems weak, and Faulkner's treatment of it verges at times on the sentimental. The version of "Delta Autumn" which forms the epilogue of Big Woods, for example, omits all reference to Ike McCaslin's encounter with Roth Edmonds's Negro mistress, and the point of the story is made to depend almost entirely upon the diminished symbolism of Roth's shooting a doe when, because of the shortage of game, he should have shot only bucks. As a result, the final rhetorical passage, which Faulkner seems to regard as of culminating importance, arises much less naturally out of what has gone before than it does in *Go Down, Moses*. In the novel the passage follows immediately upon the girl's departure and reads as follows:

> This Delta, he thought: This Delta. *This land which man has deswamped and denuded and derivered in two generations so that white men can own plantations and commute every night to Memphis and black men own plantations and ride in jim crow cars to Chicago to live in millionaires' mansions on Lakeshore Drive, where white men rent farms and live like niggers and niggers crop on shares and live like animals, where cotton is planted and grows man-tall in the very cracks of the sidewalks, and usury and mortgage and bankruptcy and measureless wealth, Chinese and African and Aryan and Jew, all breed and spawn together until no man has time to say which one is which nor cares.* . . . No wonder the ruined woods I used to know dont cry for retribution! he thought: The people who have destroyed it will accomplish its revenge.[13]

The version of this passage in *Big Woods* omits the words "Chinese and African and Aryan and Jew," and makes other slight alterations,[14] but it still does not seem to belong either to the "Delta Autumn" episode or to the book as a whole. In *Go Down, Moses*, however, the relevance of the passage is obvious—even if, like other passages in the book, it offers difficulties in interpretation.

Go Down, Moses has two major themes, the theme of white-Negro relationships and the theme of the destruction of the wilderness, and Faulkner's intention seems to have been to link them together by presenting the relation of man to the land as an index of moral stature. Faulkner's subsequent publication of *Big Woods*, exclusively devoted to the wilderness theme, seems a clear admission of the failure of this intention, while in the novel itself the failure is reflected in the intricacy and apparent confusion of some of the writing. It is not an overall failure, however: the fact that the themes have not been successfully fused does not mean that the book falls apart, simply that it is a less unified novel than Faulkner tried to make it. To study Faulkner's revisions of the stories included in *Go Down, Moses* and to compare the finished book with *Big Woods* is to realise clearly the seriousness of Faulkner's attempt to make it a novel and not simply a collection of short stories. The weakness of *Big Woods*, too, helps to draw our attention to the real strength of *Go Down, Moses*, which lies not in the stories of the hunt, important and impressive though these are, but in the powerful treatment of tragic relationships between white men and Negroes at various periods of the South's history.

These relationships are the more intense in that, in five out of the seven stories, they are between white and Negro members of the same family. The pride of Lucas Beauchamp derives largely from his awareness that he is a direct descendant of old Carothers McCaslin, one of the first men to come from the Carolinas to establish a plantation in Mississippi. Carothers McCaslin does not appear in the novel, and he is never even described, but his memory hangs over the whole book, just as his blood runs in all the major characters. Ike McCaslin, in particular, is obsessed by his grandfather and by the crimes he committed, and his repudiation of the land is an attempt, not so much to exorcise those crimes, for that seems impossible, as to dissociate himself from them.

It is not until we come to the fourth section of "The Bear" that we discover that the crime with which Ike is particularly obsessed is Carothers McCaslin's incestuous relationship with Tomasina, his own daughter by a Negro slave, an act which apparently drove the girl's mother, Eunice, to commit suicide one Christmas Day in the eighteen-thirties. It is only in this section, in fact, that we become aware, through the richly evocative device of the entries in the commissary account-books, of the full intricacy of the relationships between the white and black descendants of Carothers McCaslin. The genealogy on p. 115 may be helpful to readers who find themselves in difficulties at various points in the book. Not all the details are specifically supplied by Faulkner in the text, but they can all be deduced from it: Samuel Worsham Beauchamp, for instance, the gangster of the story "Go Down, Moses," is the son of a daughter of Lucas and Molly who has not been mentioned before, but who must be much older than Nat, the daughter who is an important character in "The Fire and the Hearth." And although Uncle Buddy wins the poker game and saves his brother from Miss Sophonsiba in "Was,"[15] perhaps Faulkner's most richly comic story, it becomes clear later in the novel that Uncle Buck must subsequently have surrendered.

The genealogy is also a diagrammatic demonstration of that repetitive pattern of McCaslin inter-relationships on which Faulkner lays such stress. The easy, warmly intimate relationships between white and Negro children are shown in successive generations: Cass Edmonds and Tomy's Turl, Ike and Tennie's Jim (though this is no more than hinted at), Zachary Edmonds and Lucas Beauchamp, Roth Edmonds and Lucas's son Henry. These last two friendships, as close as any relationship between brothers, are examined with great sensitivity in "The Fire and the Hearth," though it is perhaps a weakness of that story that these episodes become almost swamped by the rustic comedy of the still, the trial, and the gold-finding machine. Even Lucas's behaviour in these comic sections of the story, however, helps to establish his unyielding pride and his refusal to act according to the pattern which Southern tradition demands of "niggers," and which, as in *Intruder in the Dust*, Southern violence is prompt to enforce. The dark scene in which Lucas and Zachary Edmonds fight over Molly as man to man—Lucas's razor, attribute of his colour, cast actually and symbolically aside, the white man's pistol placed between them—is of central importance in the thematic structure of the novel and in the development of Lucas as a character, both in this book and in *Intruder in the Dust*, and it comes later to haunt the imagination of Roth Edmonds, Zachary's son.

Roth, worried, angry, troubled in conscience, yet still very much a Southerner of the traditional type, becomes in the novel something of a representative figure, an embodiment of the contemporary South to be set off against Uncle Ike, the still living embodiment of "the old time." Ike and Roth are seen together only in "Delta Autumn," and the scene in which Ike meets Roth's Negro mistress is the culmination of what we may call the book's inner pattern, the recurrent history of McCaslin inter-relationships, as distinct from its outer pattern, the broader themes of white and Negro relationships in the South as a whole. Roth has left Ike some money for the girl, but has not told him that she is a Negro. When the girl arrives, however, Ike soon discovers that not only is she a Negro, she is the granddaughter of Tennie's Jim, a McCaslin descendant like himself and Roth. Ike's reactions to this discovery are precisely imaged in a single paragraph:

"Take it," he said. His voice began to rise again, but he stopped it. "Take it out of my tent". She came back to the cot and took up the money; whereupon once more he said, "Wait:" although she had not turned, still stooping, and he put out his hand. But, sitting, he could not complete the reach until she moved her hand, the single hand which held the money, until he touched it. He didn't grasp it, he merely touched it—

the gnarled, bloodless, bone-light bone-dry old man's fingers touching for a second the smooth young flesh where the strong old blood ran after its long lost journey back to home. "Tennie's Jim," he said. "Tennie's Jim." He drew the hand back beneath the blanket again: he said harshly now: "It's a boy, I reckon. They usually are, except that one that was its own mother too".[16]

The "strong old blood" is, of course, that of Carothers McCaslin, and the whole scene is dominated by Ike's sense of the completion of the tragic circle of wrong-doing which old Carothers had begun, and by his awareness that his own act of repudiation has been rendered meaningless by Roth's initiation of a new onward movement through time. The last sentence, with its reference to Tomasina—she, mistress to her father, is presumably the "one that was its own mother too"—reveals how bitterly Ike is dwelling on the recurrence of the evil patterns of the past. Ike is also looking towards the future, however: by touching the girl's hand he makes a gesture of recognition which represents, for a Southerner, a violent break with tradition, but he makes it only with difficulty and the Negro has to move towards him before it can be completed.

By this act of recognition, and by presenting the child with General Compson's hunting horn a few minutes later, Ike is apparently trying, in the immediate situation, to make good his insulting insistence that the girl take the money Roth has left for her. Its wider significance seems to be that Ike has realised that he is dealing with a new kind of Negro—this girl, while still possessing the old Negro passivity, has nevertheless education, intelligence, and a sense of personal dignity and responsibility—and that the Negro can no longer be bought off, the crimes against him expiated in cash, but must be recognised, equally with the white man, as an individual and as the

heir to the best traditions of the South. But the time for
complete equality, for the mingling of the races, has not
yet come: *"Maybe in a thousand or two thousand years in
America,"* thinks Ike when he first learns that the girl is a
Negro, *"But not now! Not now!"*[17]

The tension in the whole scene derives from the complexity of Ike's reactions; for along with his anger and
sickness at the deed and his sense of personal defeat goes
compassion and even affection for the girl and child
whom he now knows to be his own kin—but also a still
unconquerable revulsion from the girl as Negro and from
the whole idea of miscegenation. It is this revulsion which
provides the violent impetus behind the rhetorical passage on the corruption of the South quoted earlier, and it
is the omission of this causation in *Big Woods* which makes
the passage appear out of context there.

Faulkner's attitude towards the contemporary problems of the South is exactly and sensitively imaged in this
scene, and the whole of *Intruder in the Dust* seems no more
than a gloss upon it. For all his goodwill towards the
Negro, for all his desire to expiate the crimes against the
Negro perpetrated by his forefathers—the misdeeds of
Carothers McCaslin become a symbol of those of the
whole South during the period of slavery—Ike can only
act within the limitations of his time, his society, and his
colour. The girl is a Negro and he is a white man: therefore, " 'Cant nobody do nothing for you!' "[18] Nevertheless, Ike rouses himself to go through the effort and
shame (" 'I aint got my pants on' ")[19] of rising from his
bed to present her with the symbolic horn. We realise
that the effort is heroic, only he cannot quite manage it:
he cannot give it to her with his own hands, but only tell
her to take it. The time is not yet.

The presentation of the horn marks a deliberate attempt on Faulkner's part to merge the wilderness theme
with the white-Negro theme, just as past and future are
merged in the person of the new-born child. The hunting-

horn, a symbol of the wilderness and of what initiation into the secrets of the wilderness means, is given up to a new generation which will not know what these things signify: " 'Go back North,' " Ike tells the girl.[20] The wilderness has almost gone—Ike is encamped in its last stronghold, two hundred miles from Jefferson now instead of thirty—and the surrender of the horn marks both its final destruction and Ike's realisation that it is not for any individual to avenge that destruction. "The people who have destroyed it will accomplish its revenge": the cynical rape of the land, like the related cynicism of slaveholding, will be avenged by the perpetual pattern of violence and retribution which the guilty Southerner imposes upon himself and his descendants.

This, or something like it, is what Faulkner seems to be saying at the end of "Delta Autumn," and it is underlined by Roth Edmonds's killing of the doe, which provides an apt image of the white-Negro theme in terms of the destruction of the wilderness. It seems impossible, however, to be entirely clear or entirely happy about Faulkner's attitude to the wilderness, or about his somewhat mystical notions concerning the impossibility of anyone ever "owning" the land. The important thing, however, as with all Faulkner's ideas, is not to let them get in the way. We do not have to accept a writer's beliefs in order to appreciate their importance for the writer himself or to recognise the validity of the experience presented in his work. Certainly we do not have to share Faulkner's mystical intuitions about the land or his social and political views on the Negro problem in order to respond to the marvellous rendering of experience which is the special richness of *Go Down, Moses*.

"Pantaloon in Black," for instance, a story related to the outer pattern of the novel but not to the McCaslin theme, is not only one of Faulkner's most moving evocations of human grief and despair but contains some remarkably precise and sensitive descriptions of physical action. In this passage, Rider, the Negro whose young wife has just died, seeks relief from his pain in the sheer violence of immense muscular exertion, and his fellow-workers at the sawmill watch him as he attempts to lift a huge log unaided:

> For a time there was no movement at all. It was as if the unrational and inanimate wood had invested, mesmerised the man with some of its own primal inertia. Then a voice said quietly: "He got hit. Hit's off de truck," and they saw the crack and gap of air, watching the infinitesimal straightening of the braced legs until the knees locked, the movement mounting infinitesimally through the belly's insuck, the arch of the chest, the neck cords, lifting the lip from the white clench of teeth in passing, drawing the whole head backward and only the bloodshot fixity of the eyes impervious to it, moving on up the arms and the straightening elbows until the balanced log was higher than his head. "Only he aint gonter turn wid dat un," the same voice said. "And when he try to put hit back on de truck, hit gonter kill him." But none of them moved. Then—there was no gathering of supreme effort—the log seemed to leap suddenly backward over his head of its own volition, spinning, crashing and thundering down the incline; he turned and stepped over the slanting track in one stride and walked through them as they gave way and went on across the clearing toward the woods even though the foreman called after him: "Rider!" and again: "You, Rider!"[21]

The verbal precision and subtle rhythmic qualities of this passage make it clear that Faulkner at this time was still at the height of his powers as a writer, and "Pantaloon in Black" is one of the finest of his short stories. And even though the evidence of *Go Down, Moses* as a whole might seem to suggest that in the years following *Absalom, Absalom!* it was only in the shorter forms of fiction that

Faulkner could find a natural and appropriate medium of expression, there is no doubt that he was actually experimenting all the while with new methods of bringing diverse materials into structural and thematic unity.

REFERENCES

1. *Scribner's*, LXXXIX (1931), pp. 585 ff.
2. *The Unvanquished*, p. 146 (288).
3. *W.P.*, p. 278 (256).
4. *P.F.*, p. 540.
5. *W.W.*, p. 133.
6. Vickery, *The Novels of William Faulkner* (1959), pp. 161–62.
7. *W.P.*, p. 82 (75).
8. *W.P.*, pp. 137–8 (126–7).
9. *W.P.*, p. 324 (300).
10. *Saturday Evening Post*, CCXIV (9 May 1942), pp. 30 ff.
11. *P.F.*, p. 226.
12. *F.U.*, pp. 4 and 273.
13. *G.D.M.*, pp. 364 (257–8).
14. *Big Woods*, p. 212.
15. Cp. *F.U.*, p. 40.
16. *G.D.M.*, p. 362 (256).
17. *G.D.M.*, p. 361 (255).
18. *G.D.M.*, p. 361 (256).
19. *G.D.M.*, p. 362 (256).
20. *G.D.M.*, p. 363 (257).
21. *G.D.M.*, pp. 145–6 (106–107).

CHAPTER V

THE LATE NOVELS

In the six years following the appearance of *Go Down, Moses*, Faulkner's total published output consisted of five short stories. When in 1948 *Intruder in the Dust* broke this virtual silence, much the longest in Faulkner's career, its polemical tone plainly marked a new development in Faulkner's work, one which became even more apparent in *Requiem for a Nun* and *A Fable*. At the same time, many of the themes and characters of *Intruder in the Dust* derive directly from *Go Down, Moses*—to such an extent that it can be considered a projection of the earlier novel's final story, "Go Down, Moses" itself—and before discussing the "committed" work characteristic of Faulkner's later period it may be as well to look at the even more striking example of thematic and narrative continuity afforded by the widely separated volumes of the "Snopes" trilogy, *The Hamlet* (1940), *The Town* (1957), and *The Mansion* (1959).

The Hamlet, which was published before *Go Down, Moses* and belongs properly to Faulkner's middle period, is not only the best novel of the trilogy but probably Faulkner's most distinguished work since *Absalom, Absalom!*. It is, of course, completely different from *Absalom, Absalom!* in every way: the structure is loose and episodic, the tone primarily comic, the style marked, for the most part, by a flexible colloquialism. Although it is intimately related to a number of short stories which preceded it, there is never any doubt that it is a novel rather than a collection of stories and episodes. Indeed, it is easy to exaggerate the extent to which *The Hamlet* has been created out of previously-published material. It incorporates, often word for word, the greater part of "Fool About a Horse," "The Hound," "Spotted Horses," and "Lizards in Jamshyd's Courtyard," together with a few pages of "Barn Burning," but these sections account together for considerably less than half the novel.

With the exception of "Barn Burning," which has been greatly altered for incorporation in the novel, none of these stories appears in the *Collected Stories*, and "Fool About a Horse" and "Spotted Horses" are self-contained "tall tales" of horse-trading which would be well worth reprinting in any circumstances. There is no question, however, of these stories being incorporated in *The Hamlet* simply for their own sakes: they are intimately related to the whole structure and pattern of the novel. In the "Fool About a Horse" episode,[1] for example, Pat Stamper and Ab Snopes engage in horse-trading primarily for the joy of the conflict and the exercise of the "artistry" involved. Set off against this encounter is the "Spotted Horses" episode[2]—considerably expanded from the original story in *Scribner's*—in which, despite the strong element of farce, there is the grim overtone of Flem Snopes's relentless rapacity in his treatment of Mrs Armstid. We see that for Flem horse-trading is not a game but purely a matter of business: the demonstration is vivid, presented in concrete terms, and it is central to the meaning of the novel.

Flem is the principal figure of *The Hamlet* and of the whole "Snopes" trilogy. The main narrative line we follow in *The Hamlet* is the story of his gradual rise through the hierarchy of Frenchman's Bend to such a position of wealth and power that he can, on the last pages, set off for Jefferson, twenty miles away, as a larger and hence more appropriate field for the operations of his acquisitive genius. For it is something like genius that Flem possesses, or at least an unswerving single-mindedness of purpose that serves him equally well in a society where rapacity and self-interest are traditionally tempered by a certain human sympathy and crude charity. Will Varner, for instance, is no less self-seeking than Flem, but as an astute political boss he seeks peace and order as an essential condition of his rule, and is therefore at some pains to make his despotism benevolent.

To Flem, with his utter indifference to the feelings of others, benevolence is a completely foreign concept. He is technically honest in a way that the Varners are not, but his scrupulous accuracy in his financial dealings is matched by his inflexibility in exacting payments as they fall due. In economic terms Flem applies modern business methods and principles to what is still, at the turn of the century, essentially a barter economy: this is the main reason for his success among adherents of the old economy who cannot rid themselves of the illusion that there are "some things even a Snopes won't do."[3] In terms of Faulkner's moral world, this is to impose an abstract pattern upon human relationships; hence Flem's "design" is life-denying and immoral in much the same way as Thomas Sutpen's. Flem, however, has nothing of Sutpen's grandeur of purpose. He remains a petty character throughout the trilogy, and the descriptions of him in *The Hamlet* have an almost Dickensian quality of physical disgust:

He rode up on a gaunt mule, on a saddle which was recognised at once as belonging to the Varners, with a tin pail tied to it. He hitched the mule to a tree behind the store and untied the pail and came and mounted to the gallery, where already a dozen men, Ratliff among them, lounged: He did not speak. If he ever looked at them individually, that one did not discern it —a thick squat soft man of no establishable age between twenty and thirty, with a broad still face containing a tight seam of mouth stained slightly at the corners with tobacco, and eyes the color of stagnant water, and projecting from among the other features in startling and sudden paradox, a tiny predatory nose like the beak of a small hawk. It was as though the original nose had been left off by the original designer or craftsman and the unfinished job taken over by someone of a radically different school or perhaps by some viciously maniacal humorist or perhaps by one who had had only time to clap into the center of the face a frantic and desperate warning.[4]

Beside this figure is set the violently opposed figure of Eula Varner, the daughter of Flem's employer, whose appearance even at thirteen suggested "some symbology out of the old Dionysic times—honey in sunlight and bursting grapes, the writhen bleeding of the crushed fecundate vine beneath the hard rapacious trampling goat-hoof."[5] Eula, even more than such predecessors as Lena Grove, is a representative of nature and beauty, at once goddess of fertility and goddess of love. She it is who marries Flem Snopes, when she is already three months pregnant with another man's child, and this grotesque union—it is hinted in *The Hamlet* and confirmed in *The Town* that Flem is impotent—becomes the focus of the novel's meaning, and of its two major moods of humour and disgust. Flem, the economic man, and Eula, the goddess of love, can be regarded as the two poles of the novel about which the other characters and their stories group themselves in one way or another. The book is full of characters possessed by either love or self-interest. Among the former are Houston, Mink Snopes, and Labove, the young schoolteacher infatuated with Eula herself, and for all of them it is a genuine possession, which they do not want, cannot understand, and try desperately to escape. The most important love story in the novel, however, and one which modifies our impression of all the others, is that of the idiot Ike Snopes, whose passion for Houston's cow is celebrated at considerable length and in rich and elevated prose, as in this description of Ike returning to the cow with the feed he has stolen for her:

He and the dog recross the lot together in the negative dawn-wash cacophonous and loud with birds. He can see the fence now, where the dog leaves him. He climbs through the fence, hurrying now, carrying the basket awkwardly before him in both arms, leaving in the wet grass a dark fixed wake. Now he watches the recurrence of that which he discovered for the first time three days ago: that dawn, light, is not decanted onto earth from the sky, but instead is from the earth itself suspired. Roofed by the woven canopy of blind annealing grass-roots and the roots of trees, dark in the blind dark of time's silt and rich refuse—the constant and unslumbering anonymous worm-glut and the inextricable known bones—Troy's Helen and the nymphs and the snoring mitred bishops, the saviors and the victims and the kings—it wakes, up-seeping, attritive in uncountable creeping channels: first, root; then frond by frond, from whose escaping tips like gas it rises and disseminates and stains the sleep-fast earth with drowsy insect-murmur; then, still upward-seeking, creeps the knitted bark of trunk and limb where, suddenly louder leaf by leaf and dispersive in diffusive sudden speed, melodious with the winged and jeweled throats, it upward bursts and fills night's globed negation with jonquil thunder . . .

She stands as he left her, tethered, chewing. Within the mild enormous moist and pupilless globes he sees himself in twin miniature mirrored by the inscrutable abstraction; one with that which Juno might have looked out with, he watches himself contemplating what those who looked at Juno saw. He sets the basket before her. She begins to eat. The shifting shimmer of incessant leaves gives to her a quality of illusion as insubstantial as the prone negative of his late hurrying, but this too is not so: one blond touch stipulates and affirms both weight and mass out of the flowing shadow-maze; a hand's breadth of contact shapes her solid and whole out of the infinity of hope. He squats beside her and begins to draw the teats.[6]

Here Faulkner's "poeticising" seems successful and appropriate. The passage is at once a stylistic *tour de force*, an extremely sensitive piece of natural description, and a deliberate attempt to transform an episode which Frenchman's Bend regards as a simple case of crude "stock-diddling" into a magical tale of true love. The whole story is an extraordinary one, and highly ambivalent in its effects. Because we can never forget that Ike is an idiot and the cow a cow, the story is in part a comic demonstration of the absurdities of romantic idealism; but the poetic language generates sympathy for Ike, and we see in his complete dedication to his beloved an ironic comment on Flem's complete dedication to himself.

It is perhaps an ironic comment on a whole society. For although Flem is the supreme representative of self-interest in the novel he is by no means its only representative. The Varners are as self-seeking as any, Henry Armstid becomes obsessed by the dream of wealth, and even Ratliff, the reasonable man and ironic observer of Snopesism, falls into Flem's silver-baited trap in the last section of the novel. And after Flem, of course, comes the apparently inexhaustible line of minor Snopeses, cousins, uncles and even obscurer connections of the original family, whose appearance is described in terms of animal imagery and whose invasion of Frenchman's Bend takes on the character of an infestation. Most of them are weak imitations of Flem, despicable money-grubbers like Lump and I.O., but they fail to emulate his success because of their inability to imitate his laconic inscrutability or to adapt themselves to their surroundings, as Flem has done in his careful imitation of Will Varner's methods, mannerisms, and clothes.

A few of the Snopes clan, such as Eck and his son Wall-street Panic, are harmless enough, however, and in Mink Snopes, the murderer of Houston, Faulkner has created a strangely compelling figure, at once vicious, pathetic, and courageously independent. The ambivalence of such figures as Mink and Ike, like the mingling of farce and near-tragedy in the stories of Eula Varner and Henry Armstid, is typical of the whole mode of *The Hamlet*. The novel contains some of Faulkner's best writing, and through its episodic structure he is able to pursue with greater complexity, yet with a much greater sense of unity, the process of juxtaposition, reflexion and accretion with which he experimented in *The Wild Palms*.

The two subsequent novels of the "Snopes" trilogy, *The Town* and *The Mansion*, make pleasant and easy reading. They give the reader no particular difficulty and no great excitement. It is impossible to write enthusiastically about them; and when Faulkner says that the trilogy is a "chronicle" rather than a novel,[7] it is difficult to tell whether this is a statement of intention or of justification. *The Town*, in particular, is relaxed, even loose, in style, and episodic in structure, incorporating reworked versions of the stories "Centaur in Brass" and "Mule in the Yard," both included in the *Collected Stories*, and summarised versions of parts of *The Hamlet*. The omniscient narrator of the earlier novel is replaced here by a triple point of view, with the action presented at various times through the eyes of Charles Mallison, V. K. Ratliff and Gavin Stevens. The possible advantages of this are qualified by the fact that Ratliff and Stevens are on the "same side" in the anti-Snopes campaign, and that Charles Mallison, Stevens's nephew, had not been born at the time when many of the events of the novel took place. It is made clear, however, that Charles is intended to represent the collective viewpoint of the town itself.

Ratliff, the sewing-machine agent who performs in *The Hamlet* something of the function of an ironic commentator, is the chief link between the earlier novel, set in Frenchman's Bend, and *The Town*; and it is possible to blame some of the many inconsistencies between the two books upon his already familiar habit of enlarging freely upon the bare facts of his stories. In *The Town*, he and Gavin Stevens regard themselves as allies in a perpetual struggle against Snopesism in Jefferson: but where Ratliff's memory of his defeat by Flem Snopes at the end of *The Hamlet* keeps him from straying far beyond his chosen role of observer and commentator—though he does act against Senator Clarence Snopes in *The Mansion*—Stevens, impetuous and idealistic, has at first no such inhibitions and enters the lists against Flem in something like a crusading spirit. In their first encounter, however, Stevens is defeated, and it becomes clear that he is hopelessly handicapped by his passion for Flem's beautiful wife and, later, by his protective love for Eula's daughter Linda.

Eula, whose beauty is celebrated again and again throughout the novel, becomes a more interesting character than she is in *The Hamlet* and takes on new stature as the representative of natural vitality and freedom, the embodiment of opposition to restraint and social forms. As such, she is the inevitable enemy of Flem, and her long relationship with Manfred de Spain is a constant threat to her husband's social position. It is a threat which Flem is able to contain, however, and even turn to his advantage, so that we watch Eula's infidelity provide the means by which Flem makes his steady ascent through the ranks of Jefferson society until he is president of the Sartoris bank, a deacon of the Baptist church, and owner of the old De Spain house, which he has remodelled to look like an ante-bellum Southern mansion. The culmination of Flem's triumph coincides with Eula's death; and though her act of suicide seems somewhat out of character, there is no doubt that it is "right" in the same way as the death of Charlotte Rittenmeyer in *The Wild Palms* seems the inevitable outcome of her brave but ultimately hopeless defiance of social conventions.

The disarming of Stevens, begun by Eula, is completed, in episodes of comic irony, by Flem himself. For Flem discovers that the quality he needs to complete his success is respectability, and that it is in his own interest to act in the name of civic responsibility to rid the town of unrespectable Snopeses who are still only interested in money. Eck's son, Wallstreet Panic Snopes, falls outside this category, for he has achieved a respectability and wealth even greater than Flem's through absolute honesty and fair dealing; and Flem's main effort is directed against Montgomery Ward Snopes, who has been running a "studio" for the display of pornographic photographs. Flem is careful, however, not simply to get rid of Montgomery Ward but to see that he is sent not to a Federal prison, but to the State prison at Parchman, and his reasons for this only become fully clear in *The Mansion*.

The Town is one of the least successful of Faulkner's books. *The Mansion*, happily, is a considerably better novel, with greater coherence and organisation, fewer shifts in the point of view, and those more obviously functional, and a more complex plot centring upon Mink Snopes, one of Faulkner's most memorable characters. In *The Hamlet* we learned of Mink's history, his murder of Houston, his subsequent trial, and the gradual dissolution of his hope that Flem Snopes would intervene to save him. In the opening pages of *The Mansion* the story of the murder and the trial is told again, with the alterations that are customary in Faulkner's references back to the first book of the trilogy, but this time Mink is presented much more sympathetically, and the action is seen from his point of view. We now learn that Mink was sentenced to life imprisonment but vowed to keep out of trouble and earn the maximum remission of sentence in order to return at the end of twenty years and kill Flem.

This scheme is interrupted and delayed by Flem's cunning. Flem's anxiety, in *The Town*, that Montgomery Ward Snopes should be sent to Parchman now becomes clear: it is in order that he can trick Mink into attempting an escape. Mink, nearing the end of his sentence, falls into the trap and is sentenced to a further twenty years. His purpose however remains unshaken; and when after thirty-eight years in prison he at last emerges, a pathetic Rip Van Winkle, into the middle of the twentieth century, he sets out at once for Jefferson. Innocently eluding all attempts to stop him, he finds Flem sitting waiting for him in the old De Spain mansion and accomplishes the revenge for which alone he has lived and worked so long. It is a strangely affecting episode. The rest of the novel, revolving upon the relationship between Gavin Stevens and Linda Snopes, is not of the same standard, but Mink's story, set in motion in the opening section and concluded in the last, is always a silent presence which keeps expectancy alive.

Flem's patient acceptance of death, like Eula's suicide in *The Town*, seems "poetically" appropriate but not quite in character with what we have seen of him previously; and the same might be said of the part Linda plays in getting Mink out of prison, in unloosing the dedicated instrument of vengeance. The supreme importance of Flem's death is that it implies the end of the Snopes era in Jefferson, and this implication is underlined by Linda's decision to give back the De Spain mansion to the only representatives of the family she can find. It seems an unsatisfactory conclusion. It may be "just" that Flem should die at the hand of a Snopes, but it seems at once too simple and too optimistic a resolution that Snopesism, having triumphed over every kind of opposition, should simply surrender at the last.

A similar optimism is to be seen in *Intruder in the Dust* (1948), first of the three polemical novels of Faulkner's late period, in which the happy outcome of a series of unhappy and highly unlikely events is apparently to be taken as a hopeful forecast of the Southern future. The novel, as already suggested, seems to have its roots in *Go Down, Moses*, notably in the character of Lucas Beauchamp, the Negro who refuses to be a "nigger," and in the episode related in the story "Go Down, Moses," in which Gavin Stevens arranges for the burial of Lucas and Molly Beauchamp's gangster grandson who has been executed in Chicago. *Intruder in the Dust*, however, displays little of the earlier novel's profound sense of the social realities underlying the tragic or comic incidents of the surface narrative. In "Was," for example, our enjoyment of the wildly comic chase of Tomy's Turl is inevitably modified by our gradual realisation that he is the half-brother of the white men who are pursuing him. In *Intruder in the Dust* everything is much more explicit and much less convincing: the society of Yoknapatawpha County which is at the centre of the novel is itself invoked in abstract terms, as in the references to its collective "Face,"[8] while the book's narrative structure is violently and improbably melodramatic.

Charles Mallison, Jr., the narrator, whom we have already met as one of the narrators of *The Town*, is accompanied by a Negro boy of his own age and an elderly white spinster in an expedition which goes out at dead of night to dig up the grave of a murdered man and so prove the innocence of Lucas Beauchamp, too proud to plead for himself, and save him from lynching at the hands of the violent Gowries of Beat Four. The theme of the book is Charles Mallison's growing understanding of his personal relationship with Lucas Beauchamp and of the complexity of white-Negro relationships as a whole, but what emerges most insistently is the high-flown rhetoric of Gavin Stevens, Charles's uncle, as he proclaims his views on the racial question. His main theme is that the South must defend its right to set the Negro free in its own time and by its own hand, and that the white Southerner and the Negro should join forces against a vulgar and materialistic North which, with whatever good intentions, is dividing the country at a time of national crisis. From the prominence given to Stevens's opinions, and the fact that the action of the novel is in part a demonstration of their validity, it is arguable that they are in some measure Faulkner's own. As such they are incisively criticised by Edmund Wilson in his essay "William Faulkner's Reply to the Civil-Rights Program."[9]

Despite the claims which some critics have made for *Intruder in the Dust*, it can hardly be considered one of Faulkner's most successful achievements. It is difficult to take the melodramatic action seriously, and it is equally difficult not to be irritated by the complexity of much of the writing. Where Faulkner is essentially concerned with the evocation of the past, as in *Absalom, Absalom!* and in the fourth section of "The Bear," his use of the long, intricate, lightly-punctuated sentence is a legitimate and often effective device for conveying an impression of arrested time, of a single moment held suspended while its full richness and significance is explored. Elsewhere, as in the Quentin section of *The Sound and the Fury*, he may use such sentences as part of a stream-of-consciousness technique. In the contemporary narrative of *Intruder in the Dust* this kind of writing seems to have little function, except in so far as it may suggest the dreamlike nature of Charles's experience.

Intruder in the Dust was Faulkner's first book for six years, but it was quickly followed by several others. In 1949 appeared *Knight's Gambit*, a collection of five previously-published short stories and one "novella," "Knight's Gambit" itself. Of all the books Faulkner has published this is perhaps the weakest. What the stories have in common is that they all involve crime and the detection of crime and have Gavin Stevens as their central character: "Knight's Gambit" is primarily the story of how Stevens came to marry the widow of a millionaire bootlegger. There are occasional characters and situations which might be moving if differently treated— Jackson Fentry in the story "Tomorrow," for example— but the detective-story convention and the persistent intrusion of Stevens as the self-appointed embodiment of justice prevents any of the stories from coming properly alive. At the same time, they are extremely poor detective-stories: Stevens, who nearly always knows the answer before the story starts, has a habit of hugging the clues to himself and of revealing them with infuriating slowness as the story proceeds.

Gavin Stevens, a character very important to Faulkner but rarely attractive to the reader, appears again in *Requiem for a Nun* (1951), where he becomes the embodiment not so much of justice as of conscience. In *Requiem for a Nun*, which is a sequel to *Sanctuary*, Faulkner takes up and develops those themes of justice, retribution and guilt which increasingly occupied his attention towards the end of the earlier novel. The "Greek" nature of these themes is emphasised by the highly formal, even ritualistic nature of the language and structure. The central action, revolving upon Temple Drake, now the wife of Gowan Stevens—who has "paid" by marriage for the sin of deserting her at the Old Frenchman place—is presented in the form of a play in three acts, complete with dialogue and stage-directions. Preceding each act is a long exercise in impressionistic history which recounts the story of the act's main setting—in turn, the courthouse at Jefferson, the state capitol at Jackson, and the jail at Jefferson. These historical sections are written in a fluid style, reminiscent of *Absalom, Absalom!*, and presumably meant to suggest the continuity of historical processes as contrasted with the ritual formality of the action which is played out against, and in terms of, this socio-historical background. For it is clear that the expository sections and the scenes of the central drama are intended to be inter-related in quite intricate ways.

"The past is never dead. It's not even past," says Gavin Stevens,[10] and this is the lesson to be learned both from the story of Jefferson and from the story of Temple Drake. The building of the courthouse is the result of nothing more honourable than the attempt of the early settlers of Jefferson to shuffle off responsibility for the loss of a piece of government property (the lock on the mail-pouch), and the taint of this original corruption never leaves it. Beyond the courthouse stands the state capitol at Jackson, beyond that the vast man-made abstraction of the United States itself—"one towering frantic edifice poised like a card-house over the abyss of the mortgaged generations"[11]—and by erecting these symbols of legality and justice men attempt to shift off their own shoulders the burdens of personal responsibility. A legal act is not necessarily a moral act, however, as the trial of Goodwin in *Sanctuary* clearly showed; and although Nancy Mannigoe is technically guilty of the death of Temple's child, the question of guilt and responsibility cannot be left there but must be traced back to its source.

It is Gavin Stevens who undertakes this task and the play section of the book is taken up with his search. Stevens had defended Nancy at her trial, despite the fact that he is Gowan's uncle, and it is he who takes Temple to the State Governor in Jackson, apparently to plead for Nancy's pardon, but actually to give Temple an opportunity to confess her own sins, to tell the truth about her past, and thus, as Stevens believes, to give meaning to Nancy's act and death. Temple admits that she had become thoroughly corrupted during her stay in the Memphis brothel and had written violent love-letters to Alabama Red, whom Popeye killed. When, eight years later, Red's brother attempted to blackmail Temple with the letters, her infatuation with Red was reawakened and fixed itself on the brother. Nancy, the former dope-addict and prostitute whom Temple had hired as nursemaid in order to have someone of "her own sort" to talk to, has strong moral and religious beliefs, and, in a flashback scene, she kills Temple's child in a last despairing effort to prevent her going off with Pete. The play ends on a moderately hopeful note: Nancy dies, but does so gladly in the hope of thereby expiating her sins; Temple forgives Nancy for killing her child and comes to realise her own inescapable responsibility for much of what has happened; Gowan, too, has realised that he is not entirely blameless, and there seems to be a possibility that he and Temple will find a measure of peace together in the future.

Requiem for a Nun contains many interesting things, and the historical "interchapters" are generally well-written and of some importance as representing Faulkner's one attempt to recount the story of Yoknapatawpha County in a continuous and reasonably succinct narrative. It is in terms of the human story, however, that the book must stand or fall, and it is impossible to feel that the play section is successful. The dialogue is stilted, the action ritualistic, and the whole episode is only forced into dramatic existence at all by Faulkner's favourite device of delayed revelation. Both Temple and Gavin Stevens know the whole story from the start; the drama consists entirely in Stevens' relentless attempts to make Temple tell the story, to confess. As Olga Vickery observes, we are confronted not with a drama but "with a Socratic dialogue possessing stage directions" in which Gavin Stevens "becomes a Socratic midwife presiding over the moral dialectic which focusses on Temple Drake."[12] Finally, many critics have felt that the whole situation is implausible, that the murder of the child is an act violent beyond all cause or acceptance, that there is a complete failure to make Nancy a credible character, and that the final emphasis on "believing"[13] is at once too simple and too enigmatic a conclusion.

At the Nobel Prize ceremonies in Stockholm in December 1950 Faulkner made a speech in which he declared his belief in man and in the future of the human race. Many sentences from this speech are incorporated into the text of Faulkner's novel *A Fable* (1954), and the whole novel is in the nature of a gloss upon this most famous of Faulkner's public statements. It is thus a "committed" novel, a book with a message, and the measure of its failure is that it does little more than make the same simple affirmations as the Nobel Prize speech at enormously greater length and with a corresponding diminution of intensity. *A Fable* is conceived and shaped in accordance with an abstract idea and intended to enforce a specific statement; the result, as with James Gould Cozzens's *By Love Possessed*, is a novel which attempts too obviously to be a great book, a crowning achievement: a work structurally complex, stylistically elaborate, but dead.

As the title suggests, the principal meaning of *A Fable* is conveyed allegorically, and Faulkner has said that his initial vision was of Christ re-born, re-crucified, and buried as the Unknown Soldier. The structure of the novel is based upon a series of parallels with the life of Christ, specifically with the events of Passion Week, and the action takes place in France a few months before the end of the First World War, when the Corporal, who is the Christ-figure, persuades a French regiment not to attack when ordered to do so. Because the Corporal's influence has spread right through the Allied trenches and even into the German lines, the whole war seems to be at an end, until a consultation between Allied and German generals leads to a resumption of the fighting and of all the formalised rituals of nationalism and war.

At the heart of the novel is the relationship between the Marshal, French commander-in-chief of all the Allied forces, and the Corporal, whom we discover to be his son. The scene in which they confront each other is powerful and moving: a genuine excitement is generated by the

conjunction of the emotional conflict between father and
son with the dialectical oppositions of argument and
belief. Such moments are rare, however, and for the most
part the novel moves upon a plane of abstraction and
generalisation, remote from any social reality. It is notable that one of the most lively sections of the novel, the
strange story of the English groom and the injured horse
previously published as *Notes on a Horsethief* (1951), is set
in the American South, and it is characteristic of the novel
that this section should be only incidentally related to the
central theme. Faulkner's habit in this novel of making
subsidiary points at inordinate length is a major cause of
the book's complexity, but even more confusing is his way
of manipulating the allegory, the Scriptural parallels,
to suit his intuitions.

Faulkner is at pains to introduce into the modern
story, however artificially, such features as the Last
Supper, Peter's Denial, Judas's Betrayal, the Crown of
Thorns, and the Crucifixion between two thieves, but he
is sometimes extremely free in his treatment of more important aspects of the story. Thus he intensifies the human
conflict by making the Marshal the Corporal's father and
consistently presenting him as a father-figure, but the
scene in which the two meet is a direct parallel to the
Biblical scene of Christ's temptation, with the Marshal in
the role of Satan. What is fairly clear is that the Marshal
and the Corporal are the opposed representatives of a
number of conflicting principles and that their conflict
can be taken to represent, say, the perpetual struggle
between force and love, between war and peace, between
adherence to a code and individual responsibility, even
between the Old Testament and the New. The dominating theme, as Olga Vickery points out in an extremely
helpful discussion of the book, is that of the conflict between authority and freedom, and it is in line with Faulkner's previous treatments of this theme—in *Go Down,
Moses*, for instance—that he weights the argument heavily

on the side of the individual, the free spirit, in his opposition to the inert weight of rigidly hierarchical military organisations committed irrevocably to wage war in the name of the Fatherland. The rebellion fails, the war is resumed, but the Corporal has achieved his martyrdom and his spirit lives on in the undying flame on the Unknown Soldier's grave and in the defiant protests that disturb the solemnity of the Marshal's funeral. Man is immortal, said Faulkner in the Nobel Prize speech, "because he has a soul, a spirit capable of compassion and sacrifice and endurance. The poet's, the writer's, duty is to write about these things."

The highly formal structure of *A Fable* and the ritualistic incantatory tone of the writing mark the most deliberate attempt Faulkner has yet made to embody his beliefs in his fiction. It was an attempt which went entirely against the grain of his previous achievement and, as such, perhaps doomed to fail. Beginning with the rhetoric of Gavin Stevens in *Intruder in the Dust*, continuing in the ritualism of *Requiem for a Nun*, the domination of the idea reaches its highest point in the abstract world of *A Fable*. In large measure this tendency towards abstraction and generalisation was a search for universality, yet Faulkner's own creation of the vividly-imagined, richly-presented and splendidly concrete world of Yoknapatawpha County should have taught him that universality is a function of a novel's intrinsic vitality rather than of its ostensible scope. *The Town* and *The Mansion*, themselves Yoknapatawpha novels, do not share this fault of abstractness to anything like the same extent, but they clearly lack the vitality, the profusion of social representation that distinguished the much earlier writing of *The Hamlet*. Certainly they are not to be numbered among Faulkner's successes, and it has to be said that nothing he has written since the Second World War will bear comparison with the great novels of the late 'twenties and the 'thirties.

It seems possible to distinguish, in broad outline, four main periods in Faulkner's work: the period of apprenticeship; the "great" period from 1929 to 1936; the middle period; and the late period, from *Intruder in the Dust* to the present day. Where the apprentice work is interesting because of what was to follow it, the work of the later period demands attention because of what has gone before and because of the importance which Faulkner's present reputation has conferred upon it. Only the work of the years 1929 to 1942 is unquestionably important and interesting for its own sake, and even here the episodic books of the middle period, notably *The Hamlet* and *Go Down, Moses*, seem successful in detail rather than as a whole. It is the work of what we have already named the "great" period, those incredibly productive seven years which began so astonishingly with *The Sound and the Fury* and ended so magnificently with *Absalom, Absalom!* that firmly and unmistakably establish Faulkner's claim to be considered a major writer.

REFERENCES

1. *H.*, pp. 30–48.
2. *H.*, pp. 275–340.
3. *H.*, p. 271.
4. *H.*, pp. 51–2.
5. *H.*, p. 95.
6. *H.*, pp. 183–5.
7. *F.U.*, p. 107.
8. *Intruder in the Dust*, p. 182 (182).
9. In *Classics and Commercials* (1950), pp. 460 ff.
10. *R.N.*, p. 92 (85).
11. *R.N.*, p. 247 (218).
12. Vickery, *The Novels of William Faulkner*, p. 123.
13. *R.N.*, p. 283 (248).

CHAPTER VI

FAULKNER AND HIS CRITICS

Only recently has it become thoroughly respectable to speak of William Faulkner as a great novelist, and there are still those ready to declare that he is, in the accepted sense of the word, scarcely a novelist at all. From the very first, critical writing about Faulkner has been sharply divisible into the adulatory and the dismissive, and the balanced middle view, which perceives in his work a greatness transcending all faults and limitations, has too rarely been heard. The sheer difficulty of Faulkner's best work is an obvious cause of this critical disagreement; another is the violence and horror of his themes, notably in *Sanctuary*, which undoubtedly presented a stiff challenge to the sensibilities of his early critics.

As early as 1932 Joseph Warren Beach was writing appreciatively of the power and technical skill of *The Sound and the Fury* and *As I Lay Dying* and speaking of Faulkner as "one of the greatest literary talents of our day," but even he was surprised at Faulkner's relative popularity, "so almost unbearably painful is his subject-matter."[1] Other critics of the early and middle 'thirties missed the power and skill and saw only the violence. Frederick J. Hoffman, in his introduction to *William Faulkner: Two Decades of Criticism*, gives examples of the most frequent reactions to Faulkner's work during this period. Most critics found something to praise, but almost all of them finally rejected Faulkner as a serious writer for one or more of a variety of reasons, depending on their particular beliefs or political commitments. The commonest charges brought against Faulkner were that he lacked political awareness or a social conscience, that he wilfully obscured by unnecessary displays of technique what were essentially simple stories and situations, and, above all, that he was a cynical exploiter of violence, cruelty, and perversion for their own sakes.

The most distinguished intelligence to be turned on Faulkner at this time, however, was that of Wyndham Lewis, who included in *Men Without Art* (1934) a chapter, sub-titled "The Moralist with the Corn-Cob," which contains the most devastating statement of the case against Faulkner that anyone has yet produced. It is not a fair essay, it is not always strictly accurate, but it is extremely effective. Lewis's particular target is Faulkner's style. He speaks of Faulkner injecting poetry to liven up the listless passages of his prose, compiles lists of his repeated use of such words as "sourceless" and "myriad," and concludes that such repetition is not deliberate but "reveals the character of this slipshod and redundant artistic machine."[2] Although Lewis refers to Faulkner's "demented" characters ("his novels are, strictly speaking, clinics"),[3] his discussion of Faulkner's "studied amateur fatalism," though harsh, contains much good sense—as when he observes of "the Player" in *Light in August*:

But I should doubt if Faulkner is the master of any systematic notion of fatality. Evidently he took a great fancy at some time to the conception of a rigid destiny controlling human life, as exemplified in the Greek Drama: and it supplies the melodramatic backbone of his books. That is all, I think.[4]

Other English critics in the 'thirties remained suspicious of Faulkner, though vaguely aware that he was a power to be reckoned with. F. R. Leavis, reviewing *Light in August* for *Scrutiny* in 1933, felt that Faulkner, though less obsessed with technique than in his earlier novels, was still too self-consciously concerned to be "modern," and that this concern perhaps reflected a basic uncertainty of purpose. Graham Greene, reviewing *Absalom, Absalom!* in 1937, still could not come to terms with Faulkner's style, but concluded a highly critical review with an acknowledgment that, when all the reservations had been made, a certain indefinable "something" remained.

The culmination of the American attack on Faulkner came in 1942 with the publication of Maxwell Geismar's *Writers in Crisis*. The chapter on Faulkner is vigorous and intelligent, but now seems essentially wrong-headed. After writing warmly of *The Sound and the Fury*, in which he finds a rich evocation of childhood experience, Geismar goes on to underestimate *As I Lay Dying*, misconstrue *Absalom, Absalom!*, and react too violently to the violence of *Sanctuary*. His central thesis is that Faulkner, totally committed to the Southern past, focusses his hatred on "the Negro and the Female," whom he uses as scapegoats for the South's defeat, and projects the offspring of these two, the vicious mulatto, as "the moronic emperor of the future."[5] There is undoubtedly a certain ambiguity in Faulkner's attitude towards the mulatto, but the argument is greatly exaggerated. Again, after speaking of Faulkner's "hatred for life"[6] in *Light in August*, Geismar concludes:

I have used the title of Maurice Samuel's penetrating study of the Fascist superstitions, "The Great Hatred," to best describe Faulkner's work as a whole. For it is in the larger tradition of reversionary, neo-pagan, and neurotic discontent (from which Fascism stems) that much of Faulkner's writing must be placed—the anti-civilization revolt which has caught so many modern mystics, the revolt rising out of modern social evils, nourished by ignorance of their true nature, and which succumbs to malice as their solution.[7]

This gross overstatement is made possible only by freely attributing to Faulkner himself the views of his characters, and by what seems an almost wilful misreading of *Light in August* which assumes that Christmas *is* a Negro, a point on which the novel is deliberately vague, and entirely ignores the positive role of Lena Grove.

Hostile critics of Faulkner, whatever justice they may have on their side, tend to spoil their case by making statements which either ignore the obvious exceptions and counter-arguments or suggest an inadequate acquaintance with the books themselves. Sean O'Faolain, in his recent study *The Vanishing Hero* (1956), is another of those who regard Christmas as unquestionably Negro, and his criticism of the inaccuracies and inconsistencies in Faulkner's work, notably in *The Sound and the Fury* and *The Wild Palms*, seems compromised by his own tendencies towards over-simplification and sweeping generalisation. O'Faolain sees Faulkner as a negative writer, projecting his own frustrations upon his characters, but his primary object is to attack the interpretation of Faulkner put forward by Malcolm Cowley in his introduction to *The Portable Faulkner* (1945), and reinforced by his editing of that volume. O'Faolain claims, with some justice, that Cowley's approach to Faulkner gives his work the appearance of a unity that it does not in fact possess. The great historical importance of *The Portable Faulkner*, however, was to make it possible, virtually for the first time, to look at Faulkner's production as a whole.

George Marion O'Donnell's pioneer essay, "Faulkner's Mythology," published in 1939, had laid down the broad outlines of an approach to Faulkner which saw him as the adherent of traditional values in a changing world. O'Donnell identified the traditional values of social and ethical responsibility with the Sartorises of the novels, and the anti-traditional values of self-interest and amorality with the Snopeses, and tried to interpret each of the novels in terms of the Snopes-Sartoris conflict. This system proved too inflexible, however, and the allegorical interpretation of *Sanctuary* quoted earlier is typical of most of O'Donnell's observations in that it provides a

valuable starting-point rather than a definitive statement. The same might be said of the place of O'Donnell's
essay in the history of Faulkner criticism, for although
Conrad Aiken and Warren Beck had written important
appreciative essays in 1939 and 1941 respectively, it was
O'Donnell's work which prepared the way for *The
Portable Faulkner*.

Malcolm Cowley's introduction to *The Portable
Faulkner* still remains the best short introduction to Faulkner's work, despite the fact that many of its insights have
since been modified by the enormous volume of Faulkner
criticism it was itself largely responsible for provoking:
Cowley tells us that when he was preparing the edition
in 1945 all Faulkner's books were out of print. The
governing principle behind Cowley's editing was his
belief that Faulkner is not so much a novelist as "an epic
or bardic poet in prose, a creator of myths that he weaves
together into a legend of the South,"[8] and that the great
bulk of his work is a contribution to the building up of
this legend. Cowley summarises the legend itself as
follows:

The Deep South was settled partly by aristrocrats like
the Sartoris clan and partly by new men like Colonel
Sutpen. Both types of planters were determined to
establish a lasting social order on the land they seized
from the Indians (that is, to leave sons behind them).
They had the virtue of living single-mindedly by a
fixed code; but there was also an inherent guilt in their
"design," their way of life; it was slavery that put a
curse on the land and brought about the Civil War.
After the War was lost, partly as a result of their own
mad heroism (for who else but men as brave as Jackson
and Stuart could have frightened the Yankees into
standing together and fighting back?) they tried to
restore "the design" by other methods. But they no
longer had the strength to achieve more than a partial

success, even after they had freed their land from the carpetbaggers who followed the Northern armies. As time passed, moreover, the men of the old order found that they had Southern enemies too: they had to fight against a new exploiting class descended from the landless whites of slavery days. In this struggle between the clan of Sartoris and the unscrupulous tribe of Snopes, the Sartorises were defeated in advance by a traditional code that kept them from using the weapons of the enemy. As a price of victory, however, the Snopeses had to serve the mechanized civilization of the North, which was morally impotent in itself, but which, with the aid of its Southern retainers, ended by corrupting the Southern nation.[9]

It was in terms of this legend—which, as a legend, does not pretend to historical accuracy—that the editing of *The Portable Faulkner* was carried out. Cowley printed no complete novels, only stories and excerpts from novels, and he included nothing which did not relate to the world of Yoknapatawpha County or to its characters.

Cowley's interpretation, possibly indebted to O'Donnell's, was itself taken up and modified by Robert Penn Warren in an important review of *The Portable Faulkner* which first appeared in the *New Republic* (12 and 26 Aug. 1946) but has since been reprinted many times. Warren insisted that Faulkner's work be understood not in terms of an exclusively Southern experience but "in terms of issues which are common to our modern world. The legend is not merely a legend of the South, but is also a legend of our general plight and problem."[10] This has now become a critical commonplace, as have many more of the statements which Warren was the first to make: statements about the importance of nature in Faulkner's work, for example, his conception of the relationship between man and the land, his attitude to the Negro, his use of humour and symbolism. The great importance of

Warren's article was that it drew attention to an aspect of Faulkner which Cowley's editing had tended to obscure, "the degree of organization within individual works,"[11] and that it suggested a wealth of topics for investigation by future critics of Faulkner.

Since these two pieces by Cowley and Warren there has been a steadily increasing volume of Faulkner criticism, and in the United States at the present time he is probably receiving more attention than any other writer, certainly than any other living writer. Little of this criticism can be said to illuminate Faulkner's work as a whole: much of it is of poor quality, and in most of the better articles the discussion is confined to particular aspects of individual books. Attempts to come to grips with Faulkner, rather than with a single book, have been rare, and successful attempts have been rarer still. Irving Howe's *William Faulkner: A Critical Study* (1952), a pioneer work refreshingly undogmatic in its approach, was long the most balanced and genuinely critical study available: though out of print and difficult to obtain, there is promise of its reappearance in a paperback edition. Neither an attack nor a panegyric, Howe's book explores Faulkner's strengths and weaknesses, not always in sufficient depth, but always with insight and judgment. He is particularly good on some of the books, such as *The Hamlet* and *The Wild Palms*, which have perhaps received less than justice from other critics, and on the whole question of Faulkner's relation to the South and to Southern tradition and myth.[12] While generally accepting Cowley's approach to Faulkner's work, he very acutely corrects the rather loose comparison sometimes made between the Yoknapatawpha novels and Balzac's *Comédie Humaine*:

In the *Comédie Humaine* a powerful directing mind molds the individual novels into a comprehensive portrait of nineteenth-century French society, and brings to bear upon that portrait a precise social point of view. Almost always in control of his materials, Balzac isolates those traits of character which reveal the status of a social class at a given moment in history. Faulkner is not nearly so often the executive artist; some of his best work results from submission to rather than control of his materials. The *idea* of society does not entice him as it does Balzac, and he approaches it only when it thrusts itself upon his line of sight. No consistent or precise social point of view runs through his work; from book to book his attitude toward the South undergoes change and modulation, often without acknowledgment and sometimes against the resistance of his will. In the end he offers less an opinion about society than a view of man.[13]

With one exception, the other book-length studies of Faulkner are not of major importance. Robert Coughlan's *The Private World of William Faulkner* (1954) is primarily a collection of Faulkner anecdotes. Ward L. Miner's *The World of William Faulkner* (1959) contains relevant material on the historical and social background of Oxford, Mississippi, but offers little in the way of literary criticism. Irving Malin's *William Faulkner: An Interpretation* (1957) pursues a narrow psychological thesis which interprets Faulkner's work in terms of his presentation of the father-and-son relationship, which Malin sees as an image of the theme of rigidity and the need to revolt against it. More helpful is *William Faulkner: A Critical Appraisal* (1951), by Harry Modean Campbell and Ruel E. Foster, an unequal book containing several good ideas too pertinaciously pursued: its discussion of Faulkner as a "primitivist" was sharply criticised by Cleanth Brooks in the course of an essay on *The Sound and the Fury*. William Van O'Connor's *The Tangled Fire of William Faulkner* (1954) is a straightforward but somewhat sketchy review of Faulkner's work up to *Requiem for a Nun*; his recent

William Faulkner (1959) is primarily a condensation of the earlier book.

Useful as Irving Howe's book is, the only work on Faulkner that can be thoroughly recommended is Olga Vickery's *The Novels of William Faulkner* (1959), to which this present study is particularly indebted. It is not at all an easy book to read, and it is not, in the full sense, a critical work—Mrs Vickery passes no judgments on the books with which she deals—but it offers cogent and extremely thorough explications of the meaning and thematic structure of each of the novels in turn. Because the book is not concerned with value-judgments it gives almost as much attention to Faulkner's "minor" works as to those usually considered major, and such books as *Pylon* and even *Mosquitoes* emerge more interestingly from this detailed treatment than from the more cursory discussions of earlier critics. The second part of the book provides a valuable discussion of Faulkner's principal themes, attitudes, and techniques, and the study as a whole seems likely to remain the major interpretative work on Faulkner for some time to come.

One of the main divergences in Faulkner criticism has been in terms of the question first posed by F. R. Leavis: "Dostoevsky or Dickens?" Leavis decided that Faulkner lacked the ordering genius of Dostoevsky and had more in common with Dickens, and many later critics have agreed with him: Irving Howe, for example, and Leslie Fiedler, in a brief but provocative article strongly critical of Faulkner's style. Other critics, however, have seen Faulkner as essentially a poetic novelist, an "epic or bardic poet in prose"—a phrase of Cowley's to which O'Faolain takes particular exception—and R. W. Flint invokes the comparison with Dostoevsky in arguing this view in his "Faulkner as Elegist." The same basic assumption about the "poetic" nature of Faulkner's achievement lies behind such work as R. W. B. Lewis's extremely stimulating interpretation of "The Bear" and

Richard Chase's too strenuous analysis of the symbolism of *Light in August*. The chapter on Faulkner in Chase's *The American Novel and Its Tradition*, with its more moderate treatment of *Light in August* and its brief but sensitive comments on *The Sound and the Fury* and *As I Lay Dying*, is one of the best among recent statements on Faulkner, though its attempt to place Faulkner firmly in a native American tradition of romance is perhaps not entirely successful.

There is an interesting chapter on Faulkner in W. M. Frohock's *The Novel of Violence in America* and various pieces on Faulkner and the Southern literary scene in *Southern Renascence*. Especially valuable for an understanding of Faulkner's Southern background are Allen Tate's two essays, "The Profession of Letters in the South" and "The New Provincialism," and W. J. Cash's historical and sociological study, *The Mind of the South*. The great popularity of Faulkner's work in France has been reflected in a number of studies by French critics, and the most interesting of these is still Sartre's article on the treatment of time in *The Sound and the Fury*. Other important discussions of *The Sound and the Fury* include the two articles by Lawrence E. Bowling, and one by Cleanth Brooks which was contributed, with three other essays on the same novel, to *English Institute Essays, 1952*. Brooks has also written well of *Absalom, Absalom!*, as has William Poirier, and another helpful study of this difficult book has recently been published by Ilse Dusoir Lind. Alfred Kazin's important essay on *Light in August* suggests some modification of the rather stern judgments passed on Faulkner, more especially on his style, in the same author's *On Native Grounds*, while Donald T. Torchiana's able article on *Pylon* and Andrew Lytle's skilful piece on *Intruder in the Dust* also deserve mention as attempts to make out a stronger case for two much-abused novels.

Finally, we have had increasingly to take note, in

recent years, of Faulkner's own comments on his work. Following the publication of a considerable number of Faulkner interviews, with Jean Stein's interview for the *Paris Review* quite the best of them, there appeared in 1959 what amounted to a volume of such confrontations. *Faulkner in the University* has been hailed by one reviewer as similar in kind and equal in importance to Henry James's prefaces, but it is hard to give the book so warm a welcome. The questions asked at the recording sessions were haphazard and often poorly phrased, and many of Faulkner's replies, made on the spot and without reference to texts or documents, are not particularly helpful. This is particularly true of his autobiographical reminiscences, splendid stories though these often make, but it applies also to many of his purely literary observations. Obviously the book cannot be ignored—many of Faulkner's remarks do clarify various difficulties in his work— but it is not of major importance.

Despite all the interviews and all the criticism it will be a long time before Faulkner's stature can be finally assessed. There has been quite enough discussion of his social and political attitudes, which are not in themselves particularly original or exciting, and the great need now is for extended and detailed examination of the writing itself, its language, syntax, imagery, and rhythmic patterns. Although the obvious difficulty of his style, particularly in some of the late work, may make it hard for readers to come to terms with him, Faulkner is not a figure to be ignored. He is a major novelist, a master of the short story, and—for all his apparent excesses of structure, language and theme—incomparably the greatest and most exciting of recent writers in English.

REFERENCES

1. Beach, *The Twentieth Century Novel* ([1932]), p. 522.
2. Lewis, *Men Without Art* (1934), p. 45.
3. *Op. cit.*, p. 49.
4. *Op. cit.*, p. 54.
5. Geismar, *Writers in Crisis* (1942), p. 180.
6. *Op. cit.*, p. 168.
7. *Op. cit.*, p. 182.
8. *P.F.*, p. 23.
9. *P.F.*, p. 14.
10. *T.D.C.*, p. 86.
11. *T.D.C.*, p. 99.
12. Howe's chapter on "The Southern Tradition" is repr. in *Literature in America*, ed. Philip Rahv (1957), pp. 409 ff.
13. Howe, *William Faulkner: A Critical Study* (1952), pp. 24–5.

DESCENDANTS OF L. Q. C. McCASLIN

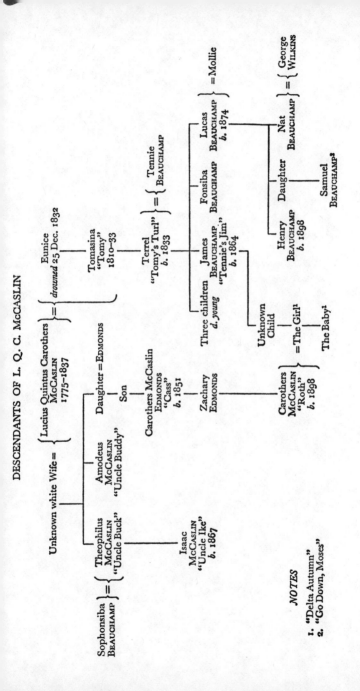

NOTES
1. "Delta Autumn"
2. "Go Down, Moses"

BIBLIOGRAPHY

I. WILLIAM FAULKNER

In the following selective list of Faulkner's works the details of American publication are based largely on the excellent bibliography by James B. Meriwether, *William Faulkner: A Check List* (Princeton 1957). For each title in § 1, the Bibliography lists the place and date of the first American and the first English edition. Wherever possible, references in the text are to editions currently in print, and where editions subsequent to the first are used they are listed in the Bibliography and marked *. Two page-references are normally given, the first to an American, the second to an English edition. The only exceptions are: *Sanctuary*, where only the Modern Library edition includes Faulkner's own introduction; *The Hamlet*, where the London text omits some ten pages at the end of Ch. I of "The Long Summer"; and, of course, those books which have not so far been published in England.

The Marble Faun. Boston 1924.

Soldiers' Pay. New York 1926. London 1930, *1951.

Mosquitoes. New York 1927.

Sartoris. New York 1929, *1951. London 1932, *1954.

The Sound and the Fury. New York 1929; with *A.D.*, in Modern Library, *1946. London 1931, *1954.

As I Lay Dying. New York 1930; with *S.F.*, in Modern Library, *1946. London 1935, *1952.

Sanctuary. New York 1930, *1932. London 1935,

These 13. New York 1931. London 1933. See also *The Collected Short Stories of William Faulkner* (1958).

Light in August. New York 1932; *[Norfolk (Conn.) 1947]. London 1933, *1952.

A Green Bough. New York 1933. Entitled *Le Rameau vert*, *Paris [1955].

Doctor Martino and Other Stories. New York 1934. London 1934. See also *The Collected Short Stories of William Faulkner* (1958).

Pylon. New York 1935, *1951. London 1935, *1955.

Absalom, Absalom! New York 1936, *1951. London 1937, *1960.

The Unvanquished. New York 1938, *1952. London 1938, *1960.

The Wild Palms. New York 1939. London 1939, *1952.

The Hamlet. New York 1940, *1956. London 1940, *1957.

Go Down, Moses. New York 1942, *1955. London 1942, *1960.

Intruder in the Dust. New York 1948. London 1949.

Knight's Gambit. New York 1949. London 1951.

Collected Stories of William Faulkner. New York 1950. London 1951.

Notes on a Horsethief. Greenville (Mississippi) 1951.

Requiem for a Nun. New York 1951. London 1953.

A Fable. New York 1954. London 1955.

Big Woods. New York 1955.

The Town. New York 1957. London 1958.

New Orleans Sketches, ed. (with intro.) Carvel Collins. New Brunswick (N.J.) 1958.

The Collected Short Stories of William Faulkner. 3 vols. London 1958. Vol. II, *These Thirteen,* contains the same stories as the original vol. of same title, whereas Vol. III, *Dr Martino and Other Stories,* contains two new stories, "Barn Burning" and "Lo!," but omits two others, both also omitted from *Collected Stories* (1950), "The Hound" and "Smoke," which had been incorporated, respectively, in *The Hamlet* (1940) and *Knight's Gambit* (1949). Vol. I, *Uncle Willy and Other Stories* (a new title), contains the other stories first reprinted in *Collected Stories* (1950).

The Mansion. New York 1959. London 1961.

II. OTHERS

See also *T.D.C.* (1951), pp. 269 ff., and Maurice Beebe, "Criticism of William Faulkner: A Selected Check List with an Index to Studies of Separate Works," in *Modern Fiction Studies,* II (1956), pp. 150 ff. — Where two editions of any work are listed, all references in the text are to the edition marked * in this section of the Bibliography.

AIKEN, CONRAD: "William Faulkner: The Novel as Form." First pub. 1939; repr. in *T.D.C.*, pp. 139 ff.

BEACH, JOSEPH WARREN: *American Fiction, 1920–1940.* New York 1941, pp. 123 ff.

——: *The Twentieth Century Novel.* New York [1932], pp. 520 ff.

BECK, WARREN: "William Faulkner's Style." First pub. 1941; repr. in *T.D.C.*, pp. 147 ff.

BOWLING, LAWRENCE E.: "Faulkner and the Theme of Innocence," in *Kenyon Review,* XX (1958), pp. 466 ff.

——: "The Technique of *The Sound and the Fury,*" in *Kenyon Review,* X (1948), pp. 552 ff. Repr. in *T.D.C.* pp. 165 ff.

BROOKS, CLEANTH: "*Absalom, Absalom!*: The Definition of Innocence," in *Sewanee Review,* LIX (1951), pp. 543 ff.

——: "Primitivism in *The Sound and the Fury,*" in *English Institute Essays, 1952,* ed. Alan S. Downer, New York 1954, pp. 5 ff.

CAMPBELL, HARRY MODEAN and RUEL E. FOSTER: *William Faulkner: A Critical Appraisal,* Norman, Oklahoma [1951].

CANTWELL, ROBERT: Introduction to *Sartoris* (Signet Edition), New York 1953.

———: "The Faulkners: Recollections of a Gifted Family," in *New World Writing 2*, New York 1952, pp. 300 ff.

CASH, W. J.: *The Mind of the South*. New York 1941.

CHASE, RICHARD: *The American Novel and Its Tradition*. New York 1957; * London 1958.

———: "The Stone and the Crucifixion: Faulkner's *Light in August*," in *Kenyon Review*, x (1948), pp. 539 ff. Repr. in *T.D.C.*, pp. 205 ff.

COLLINS, CARVEL: "About the Sketches," Introduction to *New Orleans Sketches*, New Brunswick, New Jersey 1958, pp. 9 ff.

COUGHLAN, ROBERT: *The Private World of William Faulkner*. New York 1954.

COWLEY, MALCOLM: Introduction to *The Portable Faulkner*, here cited as *P.F.* * New York 1946, pp. 1 ff. Repr. in *T.D.C.*, pp. 63 ff.

English Institute Essays, 1952, ed. ALAN S. DOWNER. New York 1954. Contains essays on *The Sound and the Fury* by Cleanth Brooks, Carvel Collins, Perrin Lowry, and Lawrance Thompson.

Faulkner in the University, edd. FREDERICK L. GWYNN and JOSEPH L. BLOTNER, here cited as *F.U.* Charlottesville, Virginia 1959.

FIEDLER, LESLIE: "William Faulkner: An American Dickens," in *Commentary*, x (1950), pp. 384 ff.

FLINT, R. W.: "Faulkner as Elegist," in *Hudson Review*, VII (1954), pp. 246 ff.

FROHOCK, W. M.: "William Faulkner: the private vision," in *The Novel of Violence in America*, Dallas, Texas 1957, pp. 144 ff.

GEISMAR, MAXWELL: "William Faulkner: the Negro and the Female," in *Writers in Crisis*, Boston 1942, pp. 141 ff.

GREENE, GRAHAM: "The Furies in Mississippi," in *London Mercury*, XXXV (1937), pp. 517 ff.

HOWE, IRVING: *William Faulkner: A Critical Study*. New York 1952.

KAZIN, ALFRED: "Faulkner: The Rhetoric and the Agony," in *On Native Grounds*, New York 1942, pp. 453 ff.

———: "The Stillness of *Light in August*." First pub. 1957; repr. in *Interpretations of American Literature*, edd. Charles Feidelson, Jr. and Paul Brodtkorb, Jr., New York 1959, pp. 349 ff.

LEAVIS, F. R.: "Dostoevsky or Dickens?" in *Scrutiny*, II (1933), pp. 91 ff.

LEWIS, R. W. B.: "The Hero in the New World: William Faulkner's 'The Bear'," in *Kenyon Review*, XIII (1951), pp. 641 ff. Repr. in *Interpretations of American Literature*, edd. Charles Feidelson, Jr. and Paul Brodtkorb, Jr., New York 1959, pp. 332 ff.

LEWIS, WYNDHAM: "William Faulkner: the Moralist with the Corn-cob," in *Men Without Art*, London 1934, pp. 42 ff.

LIND, ILSE DUSOIR: "The Design and Meaning of *Absalom, Absalom!*," in *PMLA* (*Publications of the Modern Language Association of America*), LXX (1955), pp. 887 ff.

LISCA, PETER: "Some New Light on Faulkner's *Sanctuary*," in *Faulkner Studies*, II (1953), pp. 5 ff.

LYTLE, ANDREW: "Regeneration for the Man," in *Sewanee Review*, LVII (1949), pp. 120 ff. Repr. in *T.D.C.*, pp. 251 ff.

MALIN, IRVING: *William Faulkner: An Interpretation*. Stanford, California 1957.

MINER, WARD L.: *The World of William Faulkner*. New York [1959].

O'CONNOR, WILLIAM VAN: *The Tangled Fire of William Faulkner*. Minneapolis 1954.

——: *William Faulkner*. Minneapolis 1959.

O'DONNELL, GEORGE M.: "Faulkner's Mythology," in *Kenyon Review*, I (1939), pp. 385 ff.; repr. in *T.D.C.*, pp. 49 ff.

O'FAOLAIN, SEAN: "William Faulkner: or More Genius than Talent," in *The Vanishing Hero*, London 1956, pp. 99 ff.

POIRIER, WILLIAM R.: " 'Strange Gods' in Jefferson, Mississippi: Analysis of *Absalom, Absalom!*," in *T.D.C.*, pp. 217 ff.

RUNYAN, HARRY: "Faulkner's Poetry," in *Faulkner Studies*, III (1954), pp. 23 ff.

SARTRE, JEAN-PAUL: "Time in Faulkner: *The Sound and the Fury*." First pub. in France 1939; English version in *T.D.C.*, pp. 180 ff.

Southern Renascence, edd. LOUIS D. RUBIN, JR., and ROBERT D. JACOBS, Baltimore 1953.

STEIN, JEAN: "The Art of Fiction: William Faulkner," in *Paris Review*, No. 12 (1956), pp. 28 ff.; repr. in *W.W.*, pp. 122 ff.

TATE, ALLEN: "The Profession of Letters in the South" and "The New Provincialism," in *The Man of Letters in the Modern World*, New York 1955; * London 1957, pp. 305 ff. and 321 ff.

TORCHIANA, DONALD T.: "Faulkner's 'Pylon' and the Structure of Modernity," in *Modern Fiction Studies*, III (1957), pp. 291 ff.

VICKERY, OLGA W.: "As I Lay Dying," in *Perspective*, III (1950), pp. 179 ff.; repr. in *T.D.C.*, pp. 189 ff.

——: *The Novels of William Faulkner*, Baton Rouge, Louisiana 1959.

WARREN, ROBERT PENN: "Cowley's Faulkner," in *New Republic*, CXV (1946), pp. 176 ff. and 234 ff.; in *Literature in America*, ed. Philip Rahv, New York, 1957, pp. 415 ff., and in *T.D.C.*, pp. 82 ff.

William Faulkner: Two Decades of Criticism, edd. FREDERICK J. HOFFMAN and OLGA W. VICKERY, here cited as *T.D.C.* Introd. by Frederick J. Hoffman. East Lansing (Michigan) 1951.

WILSON, EDMUND: "William Faulkner's Reply to the Civil Rights Program," in *New Yorker*, XXIV (23 Oct. 1948), pp. 106, 109 ff.; repr. in *Classics and Commercials*, New York, 1950, pp. 460 ff.

Writers at Work: The Paris Review Interviews, ed. Malcolm Cowley, here cited as *W.W.* * New York 1958; London 1959.